DEVELOPING CREATIVE & CRITICAL THINKING
Teacher's Manual

ROBERT BOOSTROM

National Textbook Company
a division of NTC *Publishing Group* • Lincolnwood, Illinois USA

Cover credits

Sequence of torus shapes projected from
four-dimensional space provided by
Thomas F. Banchoff and Nicholas Thompson at the
Mathematics Department of Brown University,
Rhode Island. The images were generated on a
Prime PXCL-5500 computer and appeared
originally in *Beyond the Third Dimension* by
Thomas F. Banchoff, published by the Scientific
American Library and distributed by
W. H. Freeman and Co., New York.

Published by National Textbook Company, a division of NTC Publishing Group.
© 1992 by NTC Publishing Group, 4255 West Touhy Avenue,
Lincolnwood (Chicago), Illinois 60646-1975 U.S.A.

1 2 3 4 5 6 7 8 9 0 VP 9 8 7 6 5 4 3 2 1

Contents

Introduction

The aim of *Developing Creative and Critical Thinking* is to help students think more reflectively, creatively, and critically by showing them how to do it. The book is guided by three assumptions about thinking. First, clear thinking results less from practicing skills than from adopting such attitudes as persistence, open-mindedness, thoroughness, and flexibility. These attitudes are discussed in Part 1 and are exemplified throughout the book.

Second, thinking is not a single process that can be divided into a series of steps. Instead, it is a family of processes that enlighten and support one another. Although the book separates creative thinking, problem solving, and critical thinking in order to help students focus on different aspects of their thinking, these categories are not separated by hard-and-fast boundaries. Problem solving is often creative, and creative thinking can be critical. Many of the activities might (with some changes in emphasis) be moved from one part of the book to another.

Third, thinking is not an activity required only in school. Creative, critical thinking that solves problems is (or at least can be) a part of everyday life. To illustrate this point, many of the exercises deal with ordinary experiences and events. The book aims to convince students that thinking well can improve the quality of their lives, that being a reflective thinker is part of being a well-rounded and happy person.

To put into practice these assumptions about thinking, the book provides activities that are intended to encourage students to acquire the attitudes necessary for careful thinking and to provide them with a variety of subjects to think about. The activities touch on all seven of the intelligences described by Howard Gardner—logical-mathematical, linguistic, musical, spatial, bodily-kinesthetic, interpersonal, and intrapersonal (see the Bibliography at the end of this manual). Although the book does not have to be used in sequence, the activities do follow a progression. Those in Part 1 introduce in specific terms the attitudes that the rest of the book aims to develop. Those in Part 2 focus on generating ideas. The activities in Part 3 focus on applying ideas, and those in Part 4 deal with analyzing and evaluating ideas.

Most of the activities are open-ended: many different answers or responses are possible. The purpose of the activities is to stimulate an exchange of ideas. Encourage your students to talk about these activities. They will find that the ideas of others enrich their own thinking.

The writing assignment at the end of each chapter (except Chapter 26, which contains six assignments) is intended to provide your students with a review of the important ideas of the chapter and to provide you with a means of evaluating students' progress.

This manual will help you use *Developing Creative and Critical Thinking* in three ways. It discusses the purposes of each activity, provides answers (or suggested responses), and lists sources that may be consulted for additional information. Because an important ingredient of good thinking is immersion in the subject, the book surrounds each activity with enough information so that students have something to think about. You are encouraged, however, to supplement this information by consulting the sources listed in the manual or other sources.

Part 1: Thinking About Thinking

This part of the book introduces students to reflective thinking, which is described in terms of purposes and strategies (or means and ends). Students will discover that to think reflectively doesn't require that they learn new skills, but rather that they use purposefully their abilities to sense and to remember. The aim is to help students see that through the application of such traits as open-mindedness, curiosity, and persistence, they can enhance their powers of thought.

Chapter 1: Reflecting

This chapter has two main purposes: first, to help students understand what is meant by *thinking* in this book, and second, to introduce to them the value of reflection.

The four uses of the term *thinking* and the idea of reflection described in Chapter 1 are derived from John Dewey's *How We Think* (Chicago: Regnery, 1971 [1933]).

The reference to Socrates and his view of the "unexamined life" can be found in Plato's dialogue, *Socrates' Defense*.

Becoming Aware

This section of the chapter deals with seeing the ordinary in new ways.

The reference to Saint Augustine and his curiosity about *time* can be found in Book XI of his *Confessions*.

When you reflect on . . . hadn't seen before? Students' descriptions of familiar television programs should get beneath the obvious, perhaps leading to some awareness of the ways that television producers (and advertisers) attempt to manipulate audiences. You might want to have your students discuss these questions before they write or have them share their answers after they have thought about the questions individually.

Activity 1.1

1. *For what sort . . . produced?*
   Students should be aware that the audiences toward which television programs are aimed may be identified by age, sex, level of education, race, etc.
2. *Are the main characters . . . want to be like?*
   Students should pay attention to the attitudes, beliefs, and habits of their favorite characters, as well as to the life-style portrayed.
3. *Are the main characters . . . special skills?*
   Again, students should pay attention to attitudes and beliefs as well as to more obvious characteristics.

4. *If the program is a comedy . . . why not?*
   These questions attempt not only to reveal the kinds of jokes heard on television and the degree to which those jokes are funny but also to help students think about their own sense of humor.
5. *What sorts of problems . . . you have?*
   This question should get students thinking about how the world of television is different from the world they live in.
6. *Are the characters . . . you are?*
   This question further develops the ideas from question 5.
7. *Describe the plot. . . . real people act?*
   Students should think about what motivates the characters to act as they do and about whether those motives are believable.
8. *Does the program use . . . mood of the program?*
   This question should help students think about something they ordinarily might not notice.
9. *Try looking . . . do you notice?*
   Watching television without sound or listening to the sound alone are other ways of making the familiar strange so as to see it in a new way.
10. *Do you know . . . when the program ends?*
    Students may never have realized the degree to which familiarity is an important part of the appeal of television.

Asking Questions

This section reminds students that what makes the world interesting is their own interest in it. Curiosity begins with people, not with things.

Activity 1.2

Study the picture . . . as many real questions as you can.
   The questions students write should reflect genuine curiosity. It is the experience of curiosity that matters. You may want to have students work together to think of questions.

Seeing Again

This section asks students what they can learn through self-reflection.
   The questions in Activity 1.3 are similar to those suggested by Matthew Lipman and Ann M. Sharp in *Philosophy for Children* (Montclair, N.J.: Institute for the Advancement of Philosophy for Children, 1980)—questions intended to encourage philosophical thinking.

Activity 1.3

> *Here is a way . . . never noticed about yourself before.*
> Students should be able to find something illuminating in their freewriting. Make sure they spend at least five full minutes freewriting—even if they think they have nothing to say.

Time to Reflect

This section encourages students to take the time that reflection requires. If you want students to start a journal (as is suggested at the end of Activity 1.4), give them some suggestions about what kind of folder to use and what sorts of things they might save in the journal.

The quotations from Thoreau come from *Walden and Other Writings of Henry David Thoreau*, edited with an introduction by Brooks Atkinson (New York: The Modern Library, 1937, pp. 43, 101).

Activity 1.4

The notebook entry should be reflective rather than superficial. This might be encouraged by your responding to the notebook entries with questions or comments.

Rethinking: A Summary

Before your students begin to plan their how-to essay, be sure they understand that they are to explain an ordinary, everyday process or activity, the sort of thing people commonly do without thinking. One of the themes of this chapter is that reflection goes beyond the obvious, and your students' essays should be examples of this theme.

Chapter 2: The Right Attitude

This chapter shows students that reflective thinking is based on openness and attentiveness. The activities allow students to experience some of the ways these attitudes work by helping them to (1) admit what they don't know, (2) look for order in the world around them, (3) listen to opinions different from their own, (4) get involved in subjects, (5) seek out the best ideas, (6) test what others tell them against their own experience, and (7) listen to their own intuition and feelings.

The quote from John Stuart Mill comes from a speech he gave at the University of St. Andrew on February 1, 1867.

Knowing What You Don't Know

This section of the chapter will help students recognize that it isn't easy to tell the difference between true knowledge and opinion. They will find out that they are wrong about things they think they know for certain.

The conversation between Socrates and Meno is recorded in Plato's dialogue *Meno*. This dialogue deals with the problem of discovering one's own ignorance.

Activity 2.1

The questions in this quiz are not special. They do not represent basic elements of cultural knowledge, nor are they trick questions. In fact, students could add to the list or subtract from it when they quiz others. The important point is to be sure that students focus on and score only those answers they are certain are correct, and to try to get some sense of the difference between being sure of something and only having an opinion about it.

You might want to have the entire class do the quiz together. Then, after going over it and discussing the results, students will be ready to try the quiz with others. (Students might enjoy sharing the results of these "surveys.")

Looking for Patterns

This section of the chapter encourages students to find alternative ways of thinking about events by discovering patterns and relationships.

The story of the young Carl Gauss is told in *Productive Thinking* by Max Wertheimer (New York: Harper & Brothers, 1959).

The story of Ian Pulizzotto (the high school math whiz) is told in "Whiz Kids" by Mary Voboril (*Chicago Tribune*, Sunday, May 6, 1990, sec. 5, p. 11).

Activity 2.2

The answers given here are only suggestions. The point of this activity is to find alternatives that make sense.

1. *Here is a problem . . . to solve this problem?*
   The problem can be seen as 9×19, or 171.

2. *Suppose you are camping . . . What could you do?*
   Solutions include using the sun, a sandglass, a burning candle, or a bowl of water that drips from the bottom at a steady rate.

3. *Here is another . . . to this problem?*
   The division by 7 undoes the addition of the numbers; the middle number, 397, is the answer.

4. *Suppose you are in a foreign country. . . . What do you do?*
   Act it out.

5. *You want to buy . . . without using a calculator?*
   Multiplying $.45 by 100 is simple—$45. Dividing that by 3 is also easy—$15. Therefore, $20 is plenty.

6. *A friend of yours . . . this trick?*

The point of using the telephone is that, while you can hear what the magician is saying, you cannot hear what "the wizard" is saying. The magician and the wizard probably have a prearranged system. When the magician asks for the wizard, the wizard begins to say slowly, "Diamonds, hearts, spades, clubs." The magician interrupts when the wizard names the right suit. The same is done with the number of the card.

Paying Attention

This section stresses the importance of tolerance.

The quotation from Voltaire appears in *The Friends of Voltaire* by S. G. Tallentyre (New York: G. P. Putnam's Sons, 1907).

Activity 2.3

The students may need help finding columns and editorials they can use as the basis of their own persuasive writing. They may also need to be encouraged to take seriously a point of view they do not believe in. Talking about the columns and editorials before students begin writing will help them think through the ideas.

Being Thoughtful

This section of the chapter shows students the difference between dealing with a subject superficially and exploring it in depth.

Activity 2.4

You may need to discuss possible interviewees with your students. Be sure students think about the point of the interview—that is, why is the interviewee interesting? What do they hope to learn from the interview?

The interviews your students conduct might be recorded and shared, or even done in class.

Using Expert Opinions

This section should help students think about why the opinions of some people are more authoritative than the opinions of others.

Activity 2.5

Which of the following . . . worth consulting?

Decisions about who is a credible source will vary according to how each character in the list is fleshed out by the students. The point is to share ideas about how one determines whether a source is credible. To carry out this discussion, it is important to make sure that students do more than argue about labels. They need to fill in why they think the doctor, for example, is or is not a good choice; otherwise, they will not be talking about the same thing.

For example, the vice president of the advertising agency that sells toys and electronic games will probably want to discourage any restrictions that might limit business. But he or she might also have insight into a child's-eye view of the world.

Checking the Experts

This section of the chapter may seem to contradict the previous section. Make sure your students understand that, though it's important to gather the best ideas about a subject, it's also important to resist accepting any idea just because an expert says so. Gathering ideas is different from believing them. All opinions need to be tested.

Activity 2.6

Making lists of information necessary to decide whether to accept the "expert's" opinion could be done as a whole-class activity. It should certainly be something that students discuss.

A. *What information . . . checks out?*

   Students may suggest such things as finding out how common are adverse reactions to the vaccine, how common are serious complications of measles, and what percentage of people who have had the measles shot get the disease anyway.

B. *What information . . . professor's course?*

   Suggestions might include comparing the average scores of those who take the course with national averages, finding out what sorts of people take the course, and seeing whether other kinds of test-taking preparation might also improve scores.

Being Open

This section reminds students that their own feelings and intuition are an important part of reflective thinking. If reflective thinking is to be productive, it must deal with things the thinker believes are important.

The passage by Dorothy Canfield is from "How Flint and Fire Started and Grew," quoted in *The Creative Process: A Symposium*, edited by Brewster Ghiselin (New York: New American Library, 1952, p. 169).

Activity 2.7

A. If you want students to keep a "thinking" notebook, discuss with them the form it should take, the sorts of things they should keep in it, and perhaps even what to call it.

B. *Write a paragraph. . . .*

   Students could share their projects with the class, especially such projects as a picture or a dance. Make sure each student understands that the purpose of the activity is to share with others a personal discovery that makes life more meaningful.

Rethinking: A Summary

When students write their inner dialogue, be sure they maintain the dialogue form. The task is to separate elements of their own points of view into two distinct personas so as to make those points of view clearer and their contrast sharper.

Chapter 3: Having a Purpose

This chapter introduces two points about the purposes that guide reflective thinking. First, those purposes cannot come from someone else—they must come from the students. Only when students' thinking aims to satisfy their own curiosity and interests can it be truly purposeful. Second, those purposes are not predetermined. They often emerge slowly and change over time.

Discovering Purpose

This section of the chapter shows students how purposes can emerge during the process of reflective thinking. The activity gives students practice in turning an open-ended task into one with a specific purpose.

The comments of Mary McCarthy and Elizabeth Hardwick both appear in *Women Writers at Work: The Paris Review Interviews*, edited by George Plimpton and Margaret Atwood (New York: Viking, 1989, p. 175, 206–8.

Activity 3.1

Although you should assist students in gathering materials for their project (magazines, newspapers, scissors, tape, glue, etc.), do not assist them in deciding what to do with these materials. The point of this activity is for each student to find his or her own purpose.

Give students an opportunity to share what they create with the bits and pieces they cut out. You should also let them discuss the questions that came to mind and the feelings they had as they struggled to find a purpose.

The Right Tools

This section of the chapter gives students a chance to think about how their environment affects their thinking and about whether the way they approach a thinking task makes it easier or harder to achieve their purpose.

The comments of Joyce Carol Oates and Katherine Anne Porter both appear in *Women Writers at Work* (p. 365, 66–67).

Activity 3.2

When you do schoolwork . . . sit or stand or lie?

In order for students to answer these questions thoughtfully, they will need to collect several days' worth of notes about how they do their school thinking.

Encourage your students to be accurate gatherers of information. The results may well show lack of purpose in some students' approach to schoolwork. By acknowledging this, they will learn more than they would by pretending to be unrealistically studious.

After the paragraphs are completed, you may want to have students discuss in class how their school and home environments affect their thinking.

Flexibility

This section of the chapter reminds students that the purpose of an object does not have to be limited to ordinary uses. The activity gives students practice in seeing familiar objects in new ways.

Activity 3.3

See how many purposes you can come up with for each item.

This activity might be done individually or in small groups. You might stimulate students' inventiveness by holding a contest to see which group comes up with the most ideas or with the most interesting or unusual ideas.

Purpose Makes Meaning

This section of the chapter shows students that their purposes shape their understanding not only of the objects around them but also of the facts and information they read and hear.

Activity 3.4

This activity shows how flexible facts or data are, adapting themselves to different purposes (and being changed by those different purposes).

You may want to discuss the data and also the questions before you have students write their answers. Make sure they understand that there are no right answers to these questions. Rather, the questions are intended to help them think, from several different angles, about the purposes this data might serve. Point out to students that in this activity they are looking at purpose from the point of view of form, theme, and audience.

1. *Where will you use . . . story about a car dealer?*

    These questions ask students to think about the form or genre of writing in which the data might be used.

2. *What point . . . feel about cars?*

    These questions ask students to think about the inferences that might be drawn from the data and about the themes that might be developed on the basis of these inferences.

3. *To whom . . . To car lovers?*

    These questions ask students to think about the audiences that would be interested in the information.

4. *What additional . . . make your point?*

   After students answer the first three questions, they may discover that their plan for using the data raises questions that aren't answered by the information they have. This would be a good sign, because it means they have found a genuine purpose based on their own curiosity.

Rethinking: A Summary

Before students begin to plan their autobiographical sketch, you may wish to discuss with them the kinds of events that might serve as material for the sketch. Because students are to tell a story, the events they describe should have a beginning, a middle, and an end. Although the aim of the sketch is to show how the writer discovered a meaningful purpose in an experience, stress that your students should concentrate on telling the story rather than on explaining the events. Help them see how they can use the story itself to reveal the unfolding purpose of the experience.

Chapter 4: Selecting Strategies

This chapter shows students why it's important to vary their thinking strategies in different situations. The activities provide practice in three very general, problem-solving strategies: gathering information, trying different points of view, and developing a procedure.

Gathering Facts

This section of the chapter gets students thinking about why they need information to think reflectively and about how they can collect that information.

   The story about John Snow and his research into the causes of cholera can be found in *The Cholera Years* by Charles E. Rosenberg (Chicago: Univ. of Chicago Press, 1962).

Activity 4.1

A. *What facts, examples, and ideas . . . each of the following?*

   To think about changing the nutritional information on food packaging, a person would need to know what information is currently given, what the purpose of the information is, whether the information can be used easily to achieve the purpose, and what additional information might be included.

   To evaluate the location of a toxic waste site, you would require facts about the sorts of wastes to be disposed of, the plans for their disposal, and alternative ways of getting rid of these wastes, as well as facts about the geology and demography of the area.

   To find out how students feel about a dress code would require surveying them with enough questions to get a good picture of their thinking (maybe they would support one form of dress code, but not another).

   To plan where to go on vacation would require facts about the sorts of activities people would like to engage in, how much money is available, how much time is available, and so on.

B. *Suppose that you are working . . . write at least three slogans.*

To make sure students don't jump too quickly into writing slogans, you might ask them first to suggest businesses they could choose and then to list some information about those businesses. This information should include not only the product or service offered but also the clientele served, the specific location, the competition, and whatever else students can think of that might help.

When students are ready to write, encourage them to use the facts to create slogans that are informed as well as catchy.

A New Point of View

This section of the chapter encourages students to be flexible in their thinking. It gives them practice in seeing things (both literally and figuratively) in different ways.

Figure 2 (Abraham Lincoln) appears in the article "Perception" in the *Encyclopaedia Britannica,* 1st edition, vol. 14, p. 40).

Figure 3 (old woman and young woman) appears in *Seeing: Illusion, Brain, and Mind* by John P. Frisby (Oxford: Oxford Univ. Press, 1979, p. 19).

Activity 4.2

A. *It is possible . . . How do you do it?*

As the hint says, to solve this, it's necessary to see that the lines that connect the dots do not have to be contained by the boundary of the dots:

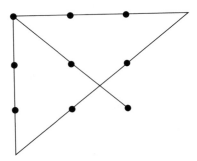

B. *Suppose you want to convince . . . How would you do it?*

The defense of sports teams should try to establish an alternative and convincing view of what sports teams are about and can accomplish, and of why they belong in school. Students might, for example, argue that schools should pass on to students more than mere "knowledge," that sports help develop character.

An Organizing Procedure

This section of the chapter shows students that trial-and-error, or guessing, isn't the best way of dealing with some thinking tasks and illustrates the difference between making a guess and devising a procedure.

Activity 4.3

A. *If you think . . . solution of the problem.*

   The cards need to be arranged like this (although it is possible to rearrange the number-suit pairings):

A♠	4♦	3♣	2♡
2♣	3♡	4♠	A♦
4♡	A♣	2♦	3♠
3♦	2♠	A♡	4♣

B. *The message below . . . figure out the message.*

   The code replaces the letters of the alphabet with the numbers from 26 to 1, "A" being 26. The message says, "Each number stands for a letter."

Rethinking: A Summary

Encourage students to make a list of books before choosing one. The book they select should be not only one they like but also one they can strongly support. After they finish the assignment, you might want to discuss with them how they used the thinking strategies in this chapter in writing their essay.

Chapter 5: Using Your Senses

This chapter encourages students to think about the relationships between perception and thought. The chapter shows that sensing and thinking depend on each other: information from the senses is shaped by the mind, and the mind is informed by the senses.

Illusions

This section of the chapter reminds students that their sense impressions are not infallible.

For more on the illusions in the first group of questions, see the article "Illusion" in the *Encyclopedia Americana*, Vol. 14 (1979) or the book *Seeing: Illusion, Brain, and Mind* by John P. Frisby (Oxford: Oxford Univ. Press, 1979).

Activity 5.1

A. If you can arrange to have the cubes of vegetables in class, students would probably enjoy seeing whether their classmates are able to tell them apart.

B. When students try the sense-of-touch test, you might have them record their results: for each patch of skin tested, they would write the number of correct and incorrect responses. Students could then share these results with the rest of the class.

C. The greater the difference in temperature between the hot water and the cold water, the more dramatic this experiment will be. After students experience the sensation of one hand feeling the water as hot while the other feels it as cold, you may want to discuss with them how the water can feel so different. The point of stress is that such sensations as hot and cold are not absolute but relative.

D. Before students check the answer to the cup and spoon illusion, you might poll the class, recording the students' estimations of the depth of the cup. This will probably demonstrate how effective the illusion is.

Point of View

This section shows students that they can change what they see and hear by adopting a different viewpoint, by looking at the world through someone else's eyes.

The excerpt is from *Adventures of Huckleberry Finn* by Mark Twain (New York: W. W. Norton & Co., 1961, p. 20).

Activity 5.2

A. *Jot down whatever details . . . different from those of your classmates?*

Students may need to be reminded that the point of comparing what people observe is not to show that some are better observers than others but rather to show that some see different things than others do. After the small groups make their lists and compare them, you may want to have someone from each group report the results.

If your students need some help with this activity, you could begin by having the whole class analyze something, such as a picture or a book cover. Students will probably be surprised at the number and variety of details that can be listed.

B. *Look around the room . . . are they different? Why?*

The lists of things observed in the room from the point of view of a toddler and from the point of view of an architect should be strikingly different. Ask students how the lists are different and list the differences on the board.

Sense and Meaning

This section of the chapter focuses on the problem of sharing sense impressions. It will help students recognize that, though conveying their sensory experiences is not easy, it can be done through the reflective use of language.

The passage by Henry David Thoreau comes from *Walden and Other Writings of Henry David Thoreau* edited by Brooks Atkinson (New York: The Modern Library, 1965 [1937], p. 206).

Activity 5.3

Then make a list of words . . . describe the event.

It might be necessary to point out to students that Thoreau's description is based not on adjectives and adverbs but on nouns and verbs. These are the words that make writing clear, specific, and vivid. Their own lists of words, created to evoke a scene, should likewise be primarily nouns and verbs.

Rethinking: A Summary

In order for students to write their descriptive essay, they'll need to spend time "in the field." Make sure that they take plenty of notes, including rough transcriptions of conversations. Stress to students that they should write down more information than they can use. In this way, they will have enough material to pack their essay full of the sensory details that will make it interesting and informative.

Chapter 6: Remembering

This chapter has two goals: first, to introduce students to some memory-enhancing strategies and, second, to show students that remembering is an aspect of reflective thinking, that it not only plays back experiences but also shapes and structures them. Remembering is creative, not mechanical.

For more on the nature of remembering, you might consult *Remembering: A Study in Experimental and Social Psychology* by F. C. Bartlett (Cambridge: Cambridge Univ. Press, 1964 [1932]).

Mnemonics

This section of the chapter contains a number of strategies that might help students not only to improve their memory but also to think about what it means to remember.

The story of the psychologist Luria and the man called "S" is told in *The Mind of a Mnemonist* by A. R. Luria, translated by Lynn Solotaroff (New York: Basic Books, 1968).

The pictorial mnemonomy for the plant classification system appeared in "Scientific Mnemonomies: Methods for Maximizing More Than Memory," by Mary E. Levin and Joel R. Levin, in *American Educational Research Journal* 27:2, pp. 301–21.

Activity 6.1

A. *Suppose you are trying . . . metatarsals, and phalanges.*

You might try using this mnemonic device by using objects in the classroom as the "hooks" on which the names of the bones will be hung. A short practice session for several days in a row will probably fix the names in most students' memories.

B. *Read the following questions . . . answers to the questions.*

You might read the questions with your students. Then, as they study the picture—without writing anything down—time them. When you review the answers, emphasize the point that knowing what to look for makes remembering details much easier.

1. *How many people . . . picture?* Ten.
   How many of them are men? All ten.
   How many are standing? Seven.
   How many are sitting? Two.
   How many are running? Three.
   How many are lying down? One.

2. *Some of the men . . . carrying or holding?*
   One is holding a machine gun, one a handgun, and two are holding suitcases.

3. *How many of the men are wearing . . . face?* Three.
   What are they wearing? Masks.
   How many of them are wearing hats? One.
   How many are wearing leather jackets? One.

4. *What do you think . . . in this picture?*
   It looks like a robbery.

C. The point of this activity is that clumping facts makes the facts easier to remember. This is why it's easier to remember a sentence than a string of words. In a sentence, only a few groups of words need to be remembered, or perhaps only a single idea. But a meaningless string of words can only be remembered by recalling each word.

D. *What other rules . . . think of?*

You might do this activity with the whole class suggesting mnemonic rules. Students may even have some rules they have devised and found useful.

If students create an interesting list, they might want to save some of the rules in their notebook, and perhaps add to the list as they think of more examples.

E. Keep in mind the idea of going through the alphabet to recall a name. The next time a student can't quite remember a name during a class discussion, suggest that he or she try this method of recall.

Discovery

This section of the chapter shows students that they know more (can remember more) than they think they know.

The Sherlock Holmes episode comes from *A Study in Scarlet and the Sign of Four* by Arthur Conan Doyle (New York: Berkley Publishing Co., 1975, p. 24).

Socrates' belief that learning is recollection can be found in Plato's *Meno*, where Socrates gives a famous lesson in geometry.

Activity 6.2

A. *Suppose you have been . . . share it with your classmates.*

You might want to walk your students through this activity. Make sure, first, that they understand their purpose is only to come up with a topic, not to write the paper. Then keep time for the whole class as the students brainstorm. Finally, lead the discussion as students share and explain their topics.

If you think your students will need help to think of topics that would fufill the assignment, you could have them brainstorm in groups of four or five, instead of having them work alone. The students in each group could then discuss their ideas and choose one, which they should share with the rest of the class.

However your students do the brainstorming, be sure that they talk about their ideas. In this discussion, also get students to talk about the ways in which one idea led to another, so that they were able to recall more than they might have expected.

If students come up with interesting topics, they should save the ideas in their notebook.

B. *Without looking at the picture . . . Use freewriting to help you recall as much as possible.*

You should have your students do this activity only if they also did Activity 6.1B.

Make sure they freewrite for a full five minutes. Like brainstorming, freewriting is a helpful way of recalling information that may have seemed forgotten, but freewriting will work only if students generate enough material so that they can make connections.

Recalling the photograph, students may realize that it's odd that none of the robbers seems to be paying any attention to the person photographing their getaway. The picture shows a film enactment of a robbery.

Memories

This section of the chapter will help students think about remembering as an act of personal reconstruction that helps them make sense of their lives and the world around them.

The excerpt by Thomas Wolfe is from *The Story of a Novel* and is quoted in *The Creative Process: A Symposium,* edited by Brewster Ghiselin (New York: New American Library, 1952).

The excerpt by Charles Dickens is from *Hard Times* (New York: Bantam Books, 1981 (1964), p. 28).

Activity 6.3

Following are three common experiences. . . . are still affecting you?

After students have recalled and written their experiences, you might ask for volunteers to share their recollections. There are, of course, no right answers for this activity. Students should discover from their own recollections, as well as from those that are shared, that it is through particular memories that such concepts as pain, conversation, and satisfaction become meaningful.

Rethinking: A Summary

Before your students begin the assignment, make sure they understand the two important characteristics of the narrative they are to write: first, the material for the incident should come from their own recollections; second, the incident should be told from the point of view of someone else. To make the point of view convincing, students will need to supplement their remembering of the events with details that might have been noticed by their chosen narrator.

Part 2: Imagining

This part of the book focuses on generating ideas. All students have the capacity to think creatively, and each of the chapters in Part 2 gives students a chance to exercise that capacity by showing them different ways to draw on and enhance their creative thinking.

The power of the imagination to reshape the world—for ill as well as for good—is discussed in the essay "Of the Power of the Imagination," in *The Complete Works of Montaigne* by Michel Eyquem de Montaigne, translated by Donald M. Frame (Stanford: Stanford Univ. Press, pp. 68–76). You might find ideas in this essay that you would enjoy discussing with your class.

Chapter 7: Creating Possibilities

This chapter allows students to speculate, to think about how changes in meaning, in the organization of parts, in point of view, and in a sequence of events lead to new ways of seeing the world, new possibilities. The spirit of this chapter is playful and, as much as possible, you should encourage your students to let themselves go.

Wordplay

In this section of the chapter, students can see how playing with words not only makes fun but also helps them to see familiar things in new ways.

The excerpts by Lewis Carroll are from *Alice's Adventures in Wonderland* (New York: Alfred A. Knopf, 1988, pp. 67, 89).

Activity 7.1

A. *What sorts of wordplay can you find in this scene?*

If you have some good readers in your class, you might ask them to read the passage aloud. Then, you could discuss the wordplay with the whole class.

Students will probably notice these examples of wordplay: "shorter hours" begins as shorter *working* hours and is taken as shorter *lunch* hour; "looking for a treasurer" is taken first as a job search, then as a missing person search; "tax" becomes "tacks"; "what do I get" is stated as a question of reward and then taken as a matter of becoming; "try my patience" is stated as a complaint, but becomes an invitation; "I wash my hands" is stated metaphorically, but taken literally.

The excerpt from the film *Duck Soup* (Metro-Goldwyn-Mayer) is quoted in *Groucho, Harpo, Chico, and Sometimes Zeppo: A Celebration of the Marx Brothers* by Joe Adamson (New York: Simon and Schuster, 1973, pp. 229–30).

B. *Working either on your own . . . more than one way.*

If your students wouldn't think it too childish, you might share with them a few examples of dialogue from an Amelia Bedelia book. Once they come up with their own examples, give them an opportunity to share their ideas with the rest of the class. They might also save their examples in their notebook. If your students do write a short story using some of their Amelia Bedelia-like expressions, you might arrange for them to share the story with the children in a second or third-grade class.

C. *Think of a playful way . . . with your reading of the headline.*
Before students think of a playful way of misinterpreting the headlines, you might discuss with them what the headlines are actually about:

- *For One Man, Solidarity . . .* refers to the divisions (or splinter groups) that arose within the Polish labor (and later political) group Solidarity.

- *Fresh Air Fund . . .* refers to the successful efforts of a group of adolescents working to reduce air pollution.

- *A One-Time Aide . . .* refers to the success of a former presidential aide as a legislative lobbyist.

- *America's Indians . . .* refers to the assumption that native Americans came to the Western Hemisphere from Asia.

- *Buzzing National Parks* refers to an invasion of bees at some parks.

When students finish their mock news stories, you might want to have some of them share their stories with the rest of the class.

Variations

In this section of the chapter, students can experiment with variations. By involving students in activities that are based on numbers, shapes, words, and actions, you can help them gain a sense of the general concept of variation and of how they can create something new and interesting by varying something old and familiar.

Activity 7.2

A. *Think of groups . . . state the rule that defines the group.*
The groups that can be formed from the numbers include the various multiples, nondivisibles, and perhaps some solutions to complicated equations. For example:

2, 4, 6, 8, 10, 12
Rule: All are even numbers.

3, 6, 9, 12
Rule: All numbers are divisible by 3.

1, 2, 3, 4, 5, 6, 7, 8
Rule: $\sqrt{n} < 3$

B. *By connecting the dots . . . two square centimeters?*

To encourage creativity, you might divide the class into small groups and have them compete to see which group can come up with the most (or most unusual) solutions. Here are some samples:

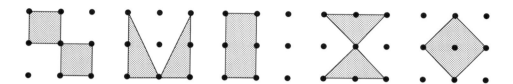

C. *Using all or some of the following, what pictures can you draw?*

You might make a display of the pictures students create.

D. *How many variations . . . the following sentence?*

After students have come up with a large assortment of variations, have them share their creations. Make sure they recognize that, although the sentences are variations on a theme, each sentence creates a unique image.

E. *Try performing . . . play the scene.*

Students can show a variety of emotions—elation, dejection, confusion, surprise, anger, love, pride, sneakiness, fear—by the way they hang the hat. You might have students perform the scene and then have their classmates guess what emotion was being expressed.

Changing Sympathies

This section of the chapter encourages students to see the world from a point of view quite different from their own.

The excerpt in this section is from *Beowulf*, translated by David Wright (Baltimore: Penguin Books, 1957, p. 44).

The novel entitled *Grendel* is by John Gardner (New York: Alfred A. Knopf, 1972).

Activity 7.3

If your students will have difficulty selecting an appropriate story to retell, discuss some possibilities with them. You may also want to show them the children's book *The True Story of the 3 Little Pigs* by A. Wolf, as told to Jon Scieszka, illustrated by Lane Smith (New York: Viking Kestrel, 1989).

You might have some students read their finished story to the rest of the class, after which you could lead a discussion about how the new point of view changed the story.

Imaginary History

In this section of the chapter, students think about the profound effects that can result from changing a small incident in a chain of events.

The examples cited are from *If It Had Happened Otherwise: Lapses Into Imaginary History*, edited by J. C. Squire (London: Longmans, Green and Co., 1932).

Activity 7.4

Think of an event . . . might have happened differently.

Make sure that students do not launch into retelling a story. Their goal should be to list the new chain of events that follows from their initial change (though you may want them later to write their ideas in a story or essay).

You might have students form small groups, with each group choosing a single historical event as the basis for an imaginary history. Students could work out a new chain of events on their own and compare their ideas with those of their classmates.

Rethinking: A Summary

Students might enjoy discussing inventions on which they could base their story. They have undoubtedly seen many such stories in movies and on television. The solid holograph generator idea has been used in the television series "Star Trek: The Next Generation." The thought-controlled computer was used in the movie *Foxfire*.

Stress that, to make their stories interesting, students must do more than just present an invention. They must show how that invention affects the lives of people. These effects are what make the story interesting, and, by thinking about these effects, students practice thinking creatively.

Chapter 8: Finding Relationships

In this chapter, students are encouraged to think creatively by looking for literal and figurative relationships. Students will think about the different ways in which ideas, words, and people are interconnected. Analogies and metaphors are introduced as ways of making new ideas. These types of figurative language are also discussed in Chapter 20, where they are used as tools for solving problems.

Analogies

This section of the chapter shows students that analogies express a relationship by focusing on one particular quality. In the activities, students get practice in dealing with the kinds of analogies that often appear on standardized tests.

Activity 8.1

A. *Fill in the missing . . . sheet of paper.*

Students will gain more from this activity if they have a chance to talk about the kind of relationship that is identified by each analogy.

1. clock : time : : scale : *weight* (The first item in the pair is a measuring device; the second item, what it measures.)

2. January : months of the year : : *Monday* : days of the week (The second item is a class; the first, one of the members of the class.)

3. bird : flying : : fish : *swimming* (The second item is the method of locomotion characteristic of the first.)

4. heart : blood : : gasoline pump : *gasoline* (The first item is a pump; the second, what it pumps.)

5. Earth : sun : : moon : *Earth* (The first item revolves around the second.)

B. *Try looking for the analogy . . . what's wrong with it.*

You may want to read this passage with your students and then let them think about it.

stop : *minute* : : stop : *Bandersnatch*

That is, the King is talking about time as if it is something you can stop the way you can stop a solid object.

This excerpt from *Through the Looking Glass* is quoted in *I Think, Therefore I Laugh* by John Allen Paulos (New York: Vintage Books, 1990 [1985], p. 8).

C. *Here are some pairs . . . complete the analogy on a separate sheet of paper.*

Sample answers:

1. child : adult : : *acorn* : *oak*

2. car : driver : : *thoroughbred* : *jockey*

3. football : quarterback : : *clay* : *sculptor*

4. bath : dog : : *homework* : *student*

5. rock : music : : *pun* : *humor*

Allusions and Metaphors

In this section of the chapter, students can practice thinking about the way in which allusions and metaphors make meaning.

The Los Angeles transit official was quoted in the *Chicago Tribune* (Sunday, July 22, sec. 4, p. 3).

Activity 8.2

A. *Listen to the conversations . . . evoke new relationships.*

Your students might find it difficult to recognize dead metaphors because the metaphors are so familiar that they no longer feel metaphorical. As a result, instead of having your students do the assignment on their own, you might want to make a list with the whole class. You could suggest examples, such as the following, to get the students started:

> She needs help; give her a hand.
> She was so excited she flew home.
> Ruth hit a screaming line drive.
> It was raining cats and dogs.
> It was a great speech; we were hanging on every word.

When your students make up new metaphors to replace these old ones, encourage the students to be original, drawing on their own experience.

B. *What does this allusion . . . that day's trading?*

If students are familiar with the movie, they will probably understand that trading was unusually wild and unpredictable. If they aren't familiar with the movie, you could make the point that allusions lose their effectiveness when people cease to recognize the reference. You might ask your students to suggest their own allusion to convey the idea.

When you discuss what the allusion conveys that straightforward language does not convey, students will probably note that the allusion adds color, life, and humor.

The stock trader referred to in this activity was quoted on the "CBS Evening News," August 3, 1990.

C. *Devote a section of your notebook to metaphors.*

If your students are keeping notebooks, they can begin collecting metaphors by recording the ones they came up with for Activity 8.2A.

Ordinary Language

This section of the chapter shows students that the act of using language is itself a way of discovering (and creating) relationships.

Activity 8.3

Here's a way. . . ordinary language.

You might want to help your students make their word lists so they don't end up with words that are too technical or obscure. After students finish the assignment, have them share what they've written.

You and the World

This section of the chapter gives students a chance to think about personal relationships. The aim is to encourage flexible thinking by heightening students' awareness of the situations of others.

The excerpts by Emerson are from "History," in *Selected Essays* (New York: Penguin Books, pp. 150, 151).

Activity 8.4

A. *You can make a map . . . in your life.*
   When you discuss this activity with your students, emphasize that they're making a map—a graphic representation of their place in the world. Their map will convey information not only by what it contains but also by how it is arranged.

B. *To explore the idea . . . the two of you are related.*
   To help your students get started on this activity, you could put names on slips of paper and let each student draw one. The students would then look for similarities between themselves and the person whose name they drew.

Rethinking: A Summary

You may want to read aloud Irving's description of Rip Van Winkle and make sure that your students see how Irving reveals the character of Rip by showing how others feel about him. Before students draft their character sketch, make sure they take the time to think about the character they're describing. They'll need to have a clear idea of the traits they're trying to portray before they can figure out how to portray them.

If students need help choosing a character, you might suggest they write about a real person or about a character from a movie or television show.

Washington Irving's description of Rip Van Winkle can be found in *Great American Short Stories*, edited by Wallace and Mary Stegner (New York: Dell Publishing Co., 1957, p. 34–35).

Chapter 9: Seeing Patterns

This chapter gives students practice in finding and creating sequential patterns and cause-and-effect patterns. The chapter shows students that thinking creatively does not have to mean spinning ideas from nothing. Making connections is also an exercise in creativity.

The passage by Stephen Jay Gould is quoted in *Uncommon Genius: How Great Ideas Are Born* by Denise Shekerjian (New York: Viking).

Sequence

This section of the chapter shows students that, to recognize a pattern, they have to understand how the pieces in the pattern are organized. This requires recognizing how the pieces are similar as well as how they are arranged. The emphasis in these activities is not on being able to predict what comes next, but on being able to explain *why* it comes next.

Activity 9.1

A. *Briefly explain . . . following sequences.*
   1. Each number is the sum of the numbers preceding it.
   2. Methods of transportation listed from fastest to slowest.

3. Methods of transportation listed alphabetically.

4. Conquerors listed chronologically.

5. Positions of the sun from equator to farthest northern position, to equator, to farthest southern position (the seasons).

6. U.S. cities from west to east.

7. Literary genres from briefest to longest.

8. The men pictured on paper money from lowest denomination to highest.

9. Closed geometric shapes from fewest number of sides to greatest number.

10. Temperatures from lowest to highest.

B. *The following sentences . . . to a different pattern.*

If your students come up with different arrangements of the sentences, you might have them explain why they think their arrangement makes a good pattern.

Sample sequence:

7. Once upon a time, a young princess went out in disguise to visit the kingdom. 9. She was dressed in the ordinary clothes of a commoner. 5. In a sack she carried a gold coin, a loaf of bread, and a length of rope. 2. Along the way, she met an old man with a sad story. 3. He said that his wife was sick, but he had no money to pay a doctor. 10. So the princess gave him the coin. 1. A little farther down the road, she met two little girls. 12. They said they were alone in the world and were very hungry. 11. So the princess gave them the loaf of bread. 6. Later, as she rested near a river, she heard someone calling for help. 8. She looked up and saw a young man caught in the river's current. 4. Immediately, she tied one end of the rope to a tree and threw the other to the young man.

Cause and Effect

This section of the chapter, which introduced the relationship of cause and effect, encourages students to look for patterns that are not obvious.

Activity 9.2

These are facts . . . What patterns can you find?

The "data" on the four school teachers is, of course, invented. One possible pattern is that the older (and perhaps more experienced) teachers are more effective, since the students of the two gray-haired teachers have aptitude scores comparable to those of the other two teachers but higher scores on the achievement tests.

Your students might find other patterns in the data. Make sure that they explain their patterns, using the facts at hand.

Stories

This section of the chapter shows students that a story is a kind of pattern. As they think about this idea, make sure they keep in mind that they themselves are storytellers and that they use this pattern-creating skill to make sense of the world.

The story about the late friend and her scientific explanation is similar to one told by J. H. Hexter in Chapter 1 of *The History Primer*—the "case of the muddy pants" (New York: Basic Books, 1971).

Activity 9.3

Read through the facts . . . why the dinosaurs disappeared.

Give your students time to think about the facts before they construct their story. You may want to have them work in groups, and then have each group report its story to the rest of the class.

The dinosaur story your students write might go something like this:

A meteorite, possibly an asteroid, crashed into Earth (bringing with it the irridium). An enormous cloud of debris was tossed high into the atmosphere where it circled the globe for years. The cloud lowered temperatures all over the world—so low in fact, that many plants that used to thrive died out. These sources of food being gone, the animals that competed for them began to perish also. In some places, the temperatures may have been so low that the dinosaurs could not survive the cold.

Rethinking: A Summary

You may want to discuss this assignment with your students and perhaps make a list of processes to help give them a sense of the possible topics.

Here are some you might suggest:

> The life cycle of a butterfly
> Human digestion
> Having a cold
> Washing a car
> A marriage ceremony

If some of your students choose complicated processes, you could encourage them to do research in the library (or field research if their subject lends itself to that).

Chapter 10: Making Meaning

This chapter encourages students to think about meaning as something that they create, rather than as something that is given. All the activities emphasize the ways in which words and symbols must be interpreted before they become meaningful.

The reference to Jules-Henri Poincaré is drawn from "The Birth and Death of Ideas" by Mary Henle, in *Contemporary Approaches to Creative Thinking: A Symposium Held at the University of Colorado*, edited by Howard E. Gruber, Glenn Terrell, and Michael Wertheimer (New York: Atherton Press, 1962, p. 35).

Names

In this section of the chapter, students are asked to think about how the words that are used to name things affect the way that people think and feel about those things. Make sure that students understand that every noun is a kind of name. The chapter is talking about all kinds of labels, not just proper names.

Activity 10.1

A. You may want to pose these riddles to your students before they read about the riddles. After your students have posed the riddles to others, have them discuss in class the answers and reactions that they receive.

    The riddles by Lewis Carroll are discussed in *This Book Is About Time* by Marilyn Burns (Boston: Little, Brown, and Co., 1978, p. 46).

B. *What do you think . . . How can you tell?*

    The headlines regarding the flag amendment are from the *New York Times* and the *Chicago Tribune*. The "house kills" headline (from the *Tribune*) makes it sound as if the House of Representatives has done a bad thing. The "amendment fails" headline (from the *Times*) makes it sound as if the amendment came up short. Students may conclude that the *Tribune* was in favor of the amendment, while the *Times* opposed it.

C. *Make a list of names . . . might refer to.*

    You may want to have students work in small groups on this activity. When they've made up lists of names and referents, have them share their creations.

    The examples "Veneering" and "McChoakumchild" appear in *Our Mutual Friend* and *Hard Times*.

Getting Inside

This section of the chapter gives students practice in interpreting words and symbols. It also shows them why interpretation is necessary.

    The formula discussed is the one the young Gauss discovered (see Chapter 2).

Activity 10.2

A. *In the first part . . . what does the* n *stand for? In the second part . . .* n *stand for?*

    In $(n + 1)$ the n means a member of a pair—the last number (which is added to the first). In $(n / 2)$ the n means the total number of pairs.

B. *Copy the passage . . . capitalization and punctuation.*

> "See it?" said the Captain.
> "No," said the correspondent slowly, "I didn't see anything."
> "Look again," said the Captain. He pointed. "It's exactly in that direction."
> At the top of another wave, the correspondent did as he was bid, and this time his eyes chanced on a small thing on the edge of the swaying horizon. It was precisely like the point of a pin. It took an anxious eye to find a lighthouse so tiny.
> "Think we'll make it, Captain?"
> "If this wind holds and the boat don't swamp, we can't do much else," said the Captain.

This passage is from "The Open Boat" by Steven Crane, in *Great American Short Stories*, edited by Wallace and Mary Stegner (New York: Dell Publishing Co., 1957, pp. 262–63).

In Other Words

This section of the chapter shows students how easily the meaning of a word (a symbol, a gesture, a style of dress) can be changed by a new context.

Antony's funeral oration is from *Julius Caesar*, Act III, Scene 2.

Activity 10.3

A. *Write a moral . . . fable illustrates.*

La Fontaine intended the fable to illustrate the foolishness that comes from allowing oneself to be flattered, but others may read the story differently. Jean-Jacques Rousseau wrote that if one identifies with the fox, then the moral will be that it pays to deceive. Rousseau's discussion appears in *Emile, or On Education,* translated by Allan Bloom (New York: Basic Books, 1979, pp. 113–16).

B. *Cut out . . . Rewrite the story in an entirely different form.*

You may want to have newspapers available so students can select their article in class. Be sure that students understand they're not paraphrasing or summarizing the article. Rather, they need to understand the essence of the article in order to convey that meaning in a new form.

C. *Choose a current fashion . . . explains its meaning.*

After your students write their paragraphs, they might enjoy sharing and discussing their thoughts, especially if more than one student has written about the same fashion. They might find that they have interpreted the meaning of the fashion differently. This would be a good opportunity for you to make the point that events, words, and actions often have multiple meanings and that searching for those multiple meanings is a big part of creative thinking.

Rethinking: A Summary

Your students may need a little priming to get them started on this topic. In dealing with their own social groups, they're writing about themselves. They may be self-conscious. Or, they may be too deeply *in* a group to be able to step outside of it with ease in order to write about it. You might get them thinking about the topic by suggesting the following group names, all of which have been commonly used by high school students to describe themselves or others:

dweebs
climbers
jocks
greasers
headbangers

When you hit upon a group that your students find meaningful, discuss the characteristics of that group, and explain that this kind of description or analysis is what their essays should contain.

Chapter 11: Predicting

This chapter shows students how they can generate new ideas by expanding on or extrapolating from what they already know.

Consequences

The first section of the chapter gives students practice in using instances of a pattern, plus a little imagination, to create a rule that helps them continue the pattern.

Activity 11.1

What comes next . . . sequences?
1. Monroe is the next president in chronological order.
2. The next number is 13; the rule is "add 3."
3. A hexagon is the next shape ($\bigcirc$); the rule is "odd numbered shape is octagon; even numbered adds one side."
4. One lollipop, stick pointed east (o—); the rule is "one pop, two pops, three pops, rotating an eighth of a turn, clockwise."
5. Wiggled; the rule is "present, past, past participle."
6. Sunshine; the rule is "sunshine every third word."
7. 1:45 A.M.; the rule is "add three hours."
8. March 22; the rule is "add 22 days."
9. The next number is 7; the rule is "add 3, subtract 2."
10. Jupiter; the rule is "planets in order going away from the sun."

Chances Are

This section of the chapter shows students how using probabilities can help them make guesses about what is likely to happen. The activities will help students see that logical, mathematical thinking plays a part in creative thinking.

Activity 11.2

A. *Is that a good payoff? . . . does it keep?*
    The payoff is not very good if you figure that, for each $1,000 you invest, you will get back only $500, because the chances of winning are 1 in 1,000. The state keeps half of the money. In comparison, casinos typically return between 90 and 98 percent of what they take in. Racetracks return about 85 percent of the money that is bet.

B. *What are the chances . . . 444 again today?*
    The chances of 444 being drawn again are 1 in 1,000, even though the chances of the same number being drawn twice in a row are 1 in 1,000,000 ($1/1000 \times 1/1000$).

C. *If you guess randomly . . . get right?*
    You will get about 25 questions correct ($1/4$).

Futurecasting

This section of the chapter shows students that genuine predictions of the future are not magical or supernatural, but rather are a matter of using what is known to make reasonable guesses about what will happen.
    The predictions about subdivisions were made by William Devereaux, Jr., speaking to the National Association of Home Builders in May 1990. The talk was summarized in "End of an Era?" in the *Chicago Tribune* (Sunday, May 27, 1990, sec. 16, p. 1).

Activity 11.3

A. *What predictions can you make . . . or rejecting it? Why?*
    Students may conclude that the end of subdivisions also means the end of malls, since neighborhoods in which homes and businesses are intermingled will probably have smaller shops. Turn down the loan.

B. *Based on what you know . . . reasons behind your prediction.*
    Make sure your students take their time with this activity. Remind them that useful predictions of the future are based on a lot of facts and experience, so they need to gather their information and think about what it implies before they start making predictions. Also stress that they are to try to predict a "big change"—one that will alter our lives or one that is surprising.

Hindsight

This section of the chapter introduces the idea that understanding the past is much like predicting the future. It calls for a combination of facts and imaginative thinking.

The idea of predicting the past is discussed in Chapter 2 of *The History Primer* by J. H. Hexter (New York: Basic Books, 1971). A humorous look at how an intentional (or historical) explanation of the past differs from a causal (or scientific) explanation appears in *I Think, Therefore I Laugh* by John Allen Paulos (New York: Vintage Books, 1985, 1990, pp. 129–37).

Activity 11.4

Based on these facts . . . people's responses to this tragedy?

You may want to discuss the story of the *Titanic* before students begin to answer these questions. Be sure students discuss their answers and explain their historical predictions.

If your students want more information about the *Titanic* or about the effects of its sinking, you could refer them to *A Night to Remember* by Walter Lord (New York: Henry Holt and Co., 1955), or *The Titanic and the Californian* by Peter Padfield (New York: The John Day Company, 1965).

Students may predict the following effects of the tragedy: (1) more precautions were taken regarding icebergs, (2) systems to keep track of icebergs were devised, (3) ships traveled more slowly, (4) lifeboats and life preservers for all passengers were required, (5) procedures for loading lifeboats were required, as were practice sessions to make sure passengers know the location of their boat, (6) smaller and less luxurious ships became more common (because insurers didn't like the risk of the larger ships).

Rethinking: A Summary

When you discuss this assignment with your students, stress the need to complete the story with an ending that fits the beginning. The ending should be predicted in some way by the beginning provided in Activity 9.1B. You might have some students read their finished stories to the rest of the class or, if possible, to elementary school students or some other audience.

Chapter 12: Combining

This chapter encourages students to think about different ways of combining facts, evidence, and details in order to generate new ideas.

Putting the Pieces Together

This section of the chapter introduces the idea that facts or pieces of evidence can be combined in a variety of ways.

The excerpt by Wallace Stegner is from ''The Town Dump,'' a chapter of his book *Wolf Willow* that was reprinted in *The Norton Reader: An Anthology of Expository Prose* (New York: W. W. Norton and Co., 1965).

Activity 12.1

A. *Use the following letters to make as many words as you can.*
   A partial list of words:

   as, at, if, is, it, ace, are, ate, ear, eat, ice, ire, its, car, cat, cafe, care, case, calf, cart, cast, fast, fist, first, last, list, lest, tea, tear, fear, sear, castle, far, fat, fit, clear, cleft, flit, stare, strife, strafe, faster, talc, tale, tile, face, fare, sate, site, sale, seal

B. *What can you learn . . . recycling center?*
   If you want your students to write about the same subject (so that they can more easily compare their findings), you might arrange for them to visit a site at your school, such as the cafeteria. However your students gather their evidence, make sure they discuss the different ways they combine the evidence to draw conclusions.

C. *What do you think . . . How do you know?*
   The cave may have been used as a bedroom, with a fire in the middle to keep sleepers warm, and with beds made of bearskins that were laid over seaweed or plants from the river.
   Stress that your students' guesses about the scene should be based on a combination of the evidence at hand.

Choices

This section of the chapter emphasizes that creative combining involves decision making. Students are encouraged to select from an array of information those facts or details that are most pertinent for their purposes.
   The example of the epidemiologist was suggested by ''A Game of Wild Indians'' by Berton Roueché, in *Eleven Blue Men and Other Narratives of Medical Detection* (Boston: Little, Brown and Co., 1953).

Activity 12.2

A. *Create your own imaginary creature.*
   You might introduce this activity by discussing the qualities needed for survival in today's world. Make sure your students understand that they should use this list as a guide to help them design their imaginary creature. Rather than writing about or drawing their creature, your students could construct or sculpt a model.

B. *Write a summary of the episode . . . imagined it.*
   Make sure your students jot down answers to the questions before they begin planning their episode. Then they can select from their notes details that will help them generate an idea.

The Unexpected

This section of the chapter shows students that combining ideas isn't an additive process: when two ideas are brought together, they're both changed. When it comes to creative thinking, two plus two often does equal five.

A discussion of the stereoscope phenomenon (and its implications for creative thought) appears in *Personal Knowledge* by Michael Polanyi (Chicago: Univ. of Chicago Press, 1962).

Activity 12.3

To experience this kind of creativity . . . invent a character . . .
This activity should help students understand that when they bring together a list of characteristics, they can imagine a person who seems almost real. After your students have created their characters and planned their stories, give them a chance to share their creations.

Rethinking: A Summary

There is no right solution to the mystery of the break-in, so make sure your students understand they can take the story wherever they want—provided the story they write uses the clues they've been given. You may want to talk about the clues with your students, pointing out, for instance, the importance of getting the facts straight—what happened and when, and who is involved. Some of your students might enjoy reading their story to the rest of the class.

Chapter 13: Classifying

This chapter looks at classifying, both as a method of making groups by combining similar instances or examples and as a method of breaking down a whole into related parts.

Grouping

This first section of the chapter encourages students to think about the bases for forming groups and about the fact that groups are created through imaginative thinking.

Activity 13.1

A. *Explain the basis . . . to group foods?*
The sources of foods along with their nutrient value determine which category foods fit into. Dividing foods into four groups gives people an easy way to make

sure they are eating a balanced diet. All sorts of other groupings are possible (and used). Terms like *junk food* and *all natural* suggest possible categories.

B. *How will you group . . . car goes where?*

Auto shows can be grouped by manufacturers, by type of car, by price range. The point is to focus on a single, inclusive quality, so that the groups are complete and mutually exclusive.

Analyzing

This section of the chapter introduces the concept of analysis as a classifying process—a way of dividing a whole to create categories or groups.

Erik Erikson's stages of life are discussed in *Identity, Youth, and Crisis* (New York: W. W. Norton, 1968).

Shakespeare's "seven ages" are part of Jaques's speech that begins with "All the world's a stage," from *As You Like It*, Act II, Scene 7.

Activity 13.2

In a few paragraphs . . . each stage different from the others.

There is no need to approach this activity as if it is a scientific study or as if there are right answers. Encourage students to have fun with the assignment and to convey in their paragraphs what they really think.

Which Ones Go Together?

This section of the chapter shows students that classifying is often a method of excluding. It also shows them that systems of classification reflect purposes. The activity helps students think about how they classify objects and people and about how they can reclassify them in countless new ways.

Activity 13.3

For each of the lists . . . different answers you can come up with.

Make sure your students not only share their classifications but also discuss them. There are no right answers, but here are some possibilities:

1. Newspaper, bulletin board, and magazine are all places to look for current events. Newspaper, novel, and magazine are things read for pleasure.

2. Rowboat, canoe, and bicycle can all be powered by one person. Rowboat, canoe, and cruise ship all travel on water.

3. Elizabeth I, William Shakespeare, and James I were contemporaries. Elizabeth I, James I, and President Bush were all heads of state. James I, William Shakespeare, and President Bush were all men.

4. Bat, telephone pole, and goal post are made of wood. Bat, goal post, and pole-vaulter's pole are sports equipment.

Bat and both poles are cylindrical.
All but bat are taller than a person.

5. All but hexagon are used for traffic signs.
   All but circle are composed of straight lines.

6. All but cheese are fruits.
   All but lime are yellow.

7. All but travel guide are standard library reference works.
   All but thesaurus can be used to find out about places.

8. All but measuring cup can be used to stir.
   All but ruler are used in cooking.
   All but spoon are used to measure.

9. All but fish are mammals.
   All but tiger make good pets.
   All but hamster are carnivores.

10. All but Foster are alphabetized under *B*.
    All but the Beatles' song were composed in the nineteenth century.
    All but Beethoven's Fifth Symphony are sung.

Rethinking: A Summary

Your students will probably have most success with this assignment if they begin not with categories of life, but with examples. Thus, they should start by imagining creatures. Then, when they've thought of at least a dozen, they can begin to think about how to classify them. Your students might also be helped by imagining the setting. What does their planet look like? What is its climate? How strong is its gravity? How many suns does it have? What is its atmosphere composed of? These factors will affect the sort of life that would develop on the planet.

Chapter 14: Breaking Habits

This chapter is about flexibility in thinking. It helps students become aware of the ways in which they limit their creativity by taking things for granted and by thinking in stereotypes, and it suggests ways of getting out of these ruts.

Methods

This section of the chapter gives students practice in thinking of new methods to achieve a given purpose.

Activity 14.1

A. *Can you solve the toothpick puzzle?*
   The toothpicks need to be in the form of a pyramid.

B. *What would be an alternative method? . . . Why or why not?*

Teachers should photocopy the maze from page 126 of the text if the students are not allowed to write or draw in their books. Because mazes are often constructed with many possibilities at the start but only one correct route leading to the finish, the fastest way to find the path is usually to start at the end and work backwards.

C. *What did the young girl suggest?*

The girl told the men to ride one another's horse.

Definitions

This section of the chapter encourages students to think about the ways in which labels and classifications, though essential for creative thinking, can also be a hindrance.

To introduce the activities, you might show the class four or five pictures of people who might be seen as counterexamples to a stereotype—a Southeast Asian woman politician, a black scholar, a white-collar criminal, a middle-aged athlete.

The reference to Galileo's work on inertia draws on Chapter 9 of *Productive Thinking* by Max Wertheimer (New York: Harper & Bros., 1959).

Activity 14.2

A. *Discuss with your classmates the old definition . . . before you could see the solution.*

The surgeon is the boy's mother. Make sure your students are aware that it is their assumption that a surgeon is a man that makes this puzzle a brainteaser.

B. *Discuss Mercier's ideas about men, women, and marriage.*

Some of your students may be included to label Mercier as sexist and, for that reason, not want to take his ideas seriously. Assure them that considering what Mercier says does not have to mean agreeing with him.

The excerpt is from Chapter 38 of *Memoirs of the Year 2500* by Louis Sebastien Mercier, translated by W. Hooper (Clifton, N.J.: Augustus M. Kelley Publishers, 1973).

1. Students may see that marriage between classes is more common and that dowries are gone. Many women are not, however, financially dependent on their husbands.

2. Mercier can see women only as homemakers and wives, obedient in all things to men. The idea that women might select (and divorce) husbands or even choose not to marry at all seems impossible to him.

3. Mercier could probably not conceive of a female surgeon.

C. *What answer to the puzzle . . . second definition?*

According to the first definition (sound as energy), sound is independent of hearers; according to the second definition (sound as sensation), sound requires hearers. Because we try to hold both ideas simultaneously, the question seems puzzling.

Goals

This section of the chapter will help students understand that, when they begin to work on a writing assignment, they don't have to know where the writing is going. They can avoid getting into a rut by letting their ideas unfold.

The excerpt is from *Back to Methuselah* by George Bernard Shaw (New York: Oxford Univ. Press, 1947, p. 246).

Activity 14.3

Choose two people . . . conversation that you hear.

To help your students with this activity, you might talk with them about people they could choose for their dialogue. Then, make sure that your students take time to get to know their two characters. You might have them jot down a few facts about each character before they begin to draft the dialogue.

Versions

This section of the chapter will help students see that their first draft (or their first thought on a subject) doesn't have to be (and probably shouldn't be) their last.

Different approaches to playing Hamlet are discussed (and illustrated with photographs) in "Tales of Hamlets Then and Now" by Richard Gilman, in the *New York Times* (Sunday, May 6, 1990, sec. H, pp. 5–6).

Studies of pigeons and their abilities to find their way home are discussed in "Complexities Rule Science" by Jon Van, in the *Chicago Tribune* (Sunday, February 25, 1990, sec. 4, pp. 1, 4).

Stephen Spender's efforts to write and rewrite a few lines of verse are described in "The Making of a Poem," in *The Creative Process: A Symposium*, edited by Brewster Ghiselin (New York: New American Library, 1952, p. 117).

Activity 14.4

Some students may try to write the last version as their first draft by combining the ideas in all the steps. Make sure your students follow the steps as described. You might even spread the activity over five days and have your students write one version each day.

Rethinking: A Summary

For this assignment, you don't want your students to write phony praise for a poem they don't really enjoy or appreciate. Make sure they understand that the purpose is to think through a response, to give themselves a chance to practice flexibility. Their thinking may confirm their negative reaction. That's all right, as long as the reaction is reflective and not just a gut response. Stress the importance of following the steps in preparation for the essay. As with Activity 14.4, you may want to spread the work over several days to be sure that students do not skip steps in the process.

Part 3: Solving Problems

This part of the book is concerned with applying creative and critical thinking to specific situations in order to come up with an answer or a solution. The activities do not provide a step-by-step approach to problem solving. Instead, they will help students understand why a situation is problematic and how they can state, transform, or reshape the problem so that they can deal with it.

The assumption underlying this part of the book is that problem solving does not involve skills or processes different from those discussed in other parts of the book. For more on this view of problem solving, you might look at *to think* by Frank Smith (New York: Teachers College Press, 1990).

Chapter 15: Defining Problems

This chapter introduces the idea that students must define their problems for themselves. Whether a situation is problematic depends on who's thinking about it.

What's the Difficulty?

This section of the chapter encourages students to think about the kinds of underlying difficulties that cause situations to be seen as problems.

Activity 15.1

Read the situations . . . what you think the difficulty is.

Sample Answers:

1. From the management's point of view, the difficulty arises from the tension between wanting people to be able to get tickets to the game and not having enough tickets for everyone. From a fan's point of view, the difficulty arises from feeling cheated out of a chance for tickets unless the system of distribution really gives everyone an equal opportunity.

2. (This situation is an actual case.) The university's difficulty is whether it can accommodate a student with acute sensitivities without giving her a special privilege that other students are denied. The student's difficulty lies in deciding what actions compromise her moral beliefs and then in determining what influence her moral beliefs should have in shaping the policy of the university's veterinary medicine department.

Getting the Facts

This section of the chapter shows students that getting facts about a problem helps them to understand the problem and to state it clearly.

Activity 15.2

For each of the following . . . decide if there is a problem.

Sample answers:

1. To assess the phone company's offer, you must consider how much you now pay for long-distance service, what percentage of those calls are out-of-state, and whether you would be willing to make them at night or on the weekend.

2. To assess the changes in the terrarium, you have to ask what outcomes would be expected: under the conditions of the terrarium, what would ordinarily happen to these organisms? Also, you should ask where the terrarium was placed, how tightly it was sealed, whether it was watered or cared for in any other way. The answers to such questions bear on the outcomes that might be expected.

An Open Question

This section of the chapter shows students that if they define a problem too narrowly, the definition can prevent them from thinking creatively about the problem.

Activity 15.3

A. You may want to help your students select characters for this game. You could, for instance, have the students choose people they have been reading about in class. However the characters are selected, make sure the students are knowledgeable enough to be able to answer the opposing team's questions about the character. After the game is over, you might ask the students to think about which of their questions were most helpful.

B. *Think about another problem . . . to define the problem.*
   Traffic congestion might be seen as a problem of

too many cars on the road

people too intent on personal transportation

not enough highways

poorly planned communities

poorly designed cars

poorly designed public transportation

After your students have thought of a number of ways of defining this problem, make sure they discuss how the different formulations point toward different solutions. You might point out that focusing exclusively on any one way of defining the problem makes it harder to think of alternative solutions.

Rethinking: A Summary

To help your students prepare for this assignment, you might ask them to think together about possible topics. Stress that they should choose a topic about which they know enough to be able to define the problem with clarity and open-mindedness. If some of the students write good letters about local issues, encourage them to send their letters to the local newspaper.

Chapter 16: Setting Goals

This chapter shows students how they can work toward solving a problem by setting intermediate, flexible goals. In this sense, a goal is not a solution to a problem but rather a target at which students aim in order to get closer to the solution.

Big into Little

The first section of the chapter introduces the idea that often the best way to solve a complicated problem is to break it down into steps or stages, thus avoiding having to solve the whole problem all at once.

Paul Engleman, the mystery writer discussed in this section, is the author of *Dead in Centerfield*. He was interviewed by Barbara Szul for the feature "First Person," in the *Chicago Tribune Magazine* (February 11, 1990, p. 52).

Activity 16.1

A. *Arrange all ten pieces to form a single square.*
   The pieces have to be arranged as follows:

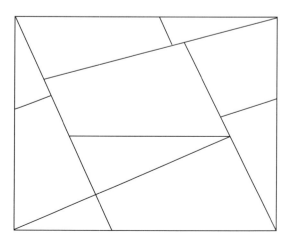

B. *How could you break . . . before you begin writing?*
   Make sure your students understand that their primary objective is not to write a limerick but to think about how to approach that task. They will probably discover at least two goals: to decide what the subject will be (in particular, the joke), and to plan the rhymes (the joke, which must be made at the final rhyme, must fit line 1).

Alternatives

This section of the chapter shows students that, because a problem can often be solved in a variety of ways, setting a goal can be a matter of choosing the best way, or the most efficient, or the least expensive. Students should see that setting a goal requires flexibility (so as not to exclude alternatives) and evaluative reflection.
   The "Star Trek" special-effects problem was described in "Special Effects Take on Special Meaning on TV" by Edward Silver, in the *New York Times* (Sunday, November 11, 1990, sec. 2, pp. 35, 43).

Activity 16.2

A. *Make a list of things you want in a college.*
   To make sure your students give this question some thought, you might time their brainstorming and emphasize the importance of coming up with as many ideas as possible within the time limit. If you need to prime their thinking, you might suggest these considerations:

> A particular course of study
> A large student body
> A small student body
> Rural setting
> Urban setting
> Friends in attendance

   When the lists have been finished, each group could report to the rest of the class. Students should decide individually, however, which considerations are most important for choosing their college. Essays explaining these personal decisions might be saved in students' notebooks.

B. *List the points . . . Then write your slogan.*
   As with Activity 16.2A, students might work best in small groups—at least while they're listing key words and ideas. If you need to prime their thinking, you might suggest that they begin by listing things that can be recycled (bottles, cans, plastic and paper bags, motor oil, cloth diapers, etc.) as well as the benefits of this recycling (saving natural resources, reducing the amount of garbage, making the environment cleaner).

Changing Goals

This section of the chapter shows students that sometimes one goal must be abandoned in favor of another if a problem is to be solved.

Activity 16.3

A. *What other headings could you look under?*
   Sample answers:

   1. *optical illusions:* perception, illusion, vision

   2. *commanders of armies during the Civil War:* Civil War, United States of America, Grant, Lee, Sherman, Jackson

   3. *the history of rock music:* music, popular music, guitars, rock and roll

   4. *how the common cold is spread:* infectious disease, viruses, respiratory disease, rhinovirus

   5. *the "studio system" of making movies in Hollywood during the 1930s:* Hollywood, filmmaking, movies, Goldwyn

B. *You've been asked to write a limerick . . . what can you do?*
   The limerick can't work without getting rid of *silver*, which has no rhyme in English. Sample:

   There once was a sorceress named Nell
   Who cast only one magic spell.
   With a toss of her hair,
   She vanished, but where
   She went, I'm afraid no one can tell.

Rethinking: A Summary

As you discuss this assignment with your students, stress that their aim is to help the letter writer break down the complex problem of being overweight, shy, and afraid to do things. Your students should seek to give the letter writer attainable goals. You may even want to discuss some suggestions with your students, such as the letter writer's analyzing his or her eating habits or beginning an exercise program. Make sure your students understand that it won't help simply to tell the letter writer to change.

Chapter 17: Representing Information

This chapter helps students think about the different ways in which the facts of a problem can be formulated, or represented. The chapter also discusses finding the most advantageous representation of facts for solving a given problem.

New Terms

This section of the chapter, dealing with mathematical representations, shows students that such representations can be a convenient way of handling information when the problem is concerned with measurement.

Activity 17.1

A. *How fast . . . for the entire round trip?*

This classic brainteaser can't be solved: no matter how fast the bus travels, it cannot average 60 miles per hour. To do that, it would have to make the round trip in one hour, and that much time passes on the outward-bound part of the journey (a fact that will become obvious to students when they try to put the facts into the formula for speed: distance divided by time).

B. *In order to know how much . . . What is your answer?*

The frames are 17 inches high (13 inches for the picture plus 2 inches on the top and 2 inches on the bottom for the frame) and 14 inches across (10 inches for the picture plus 2 inches on either side). The total area ($17'' \times 14''$) is 238 square inches. The area of the picture is $10'' \times 13''$, or 130 square inches. The difference between the two, 108 square inches, is the surface area of each frame. For a dozen frames, lacquer would be needed to cover 12×108 square inches, or 1,296 square inches (or 9 square feet, or 1 square yard).

Keeping Track

This section of the chapter shows students how they can graphically organize information that would be too complicated to hold in their heads all at once.

Activity 17.2

Use the following clues . . . from oldest to youngest.

The order of the children from oldest to youngest is Phil (swimming), Diane (archery), Elizabeth (soccer), David (basketball), and Ramona (volleyball).

Models

In this section of the chapter, students practice thinking about how they can use physical models to solve problems.

Franklin's experiments with canal boats are described in a letter to Sir John Pringle dated May 10, 1768, and quoted in *The Papers of Benjamin Franklin*, vol. 15, edited by William B. Willcox (New Haven: Yale Univ. Press, 1972).

Biosphere II was the subject of the article "An Ark for Our Future" by Georgia Tasker (*Chicago Tribune*, Sunday, February 25, 1990, sec. 5, pp. 1, 9).

Activity 17.3

A. *Think of a model . . . and demonstrate it.*

The model to find the path of an object dropped from an airplane might take many forms. Encourage your students to think of ordinary materials they might use for their demonstration. For example, a simple (though perhaps not very reliable) experiment would consist of a person running (or rolling, as on skates) toward a target on the floor. Above the center of the target would be a string hanging from the ceiling. The experimenter would drop an object (say, a pencil) when his or her arm touched the string, and an observer could note where the pencil landed. Stress to your students that their main objective is to create a convincing demonstration, not to come up with a particular answer.

B. *Come up with a problem . . . could help you solve.*

Numerous problems might be tested in Biosphere II. The interrelation of any pair (or more) of species (plant or animal) might be tested, as might the effects of different food sources on the development of a species, the rates of erosion under given circumstances, or the effects of plant growth and animal or insect life on the dome structures that might be used for colonies in space.

Rethinking: A Summary

Make sure your students understand that the challenge of this assignment lies in handling the information they collect. Before they begin questioning anyone, they should think about what they're going to record and how they're going to record it. They may, for example, want to keep track of the age and sex of their respondents as well as of the answers given. This planning will help students gather information, but they'll still have to decide how to present what they've gathered. The presentation of the data is not something that can be planned in advance: students will have to reflect on what they found out in order to decide how best to portray it.

Chapter 18: Making Progress

This chapter helps students think about what makes problems problematic. The activities give students practice with four strategies for dealing with problems that may seem unsolvable.

A Different Angle

This section of the chapter introduces a concept that has been called "lateral thinking" and shows them how to reframe a problem in order to discover a solution.

The story of the merchant and his daughter comes from *NEW THINK: The Use of Lateral Thinking in the Generation of New Ideas* by Edward de Bono (London: Jonathan Cape, 1967, p. 11).

Activity 18.1

How can the merchant's daughter . . . give her?

The girl should pick out one of the pebbles and accidentally drop it on the ground, saying that the moneylender can see what color she drew by checking the pebble still in the bag.

Activity 18.2

What would you have suggested that they do?

This might be a good activity for your students to work on in small groups. Each group could come up with a suggestion, and then the groups could compare their ideas.

The story is from *Productive Thinking* by Max Wertheimer (New York: Harper & Brothers, 1959, p. 172). Wertheimer says that the boys changed the game to one of how long they could keep the bird going.

Playing

This section of the chapter shows students that there are times when trial-and-error can be a useful problem-solving tool.

Activity 18.3

Finish the magic square.

6	7	2
1	5	9
8	3	4

Activity 18.4

By using . . . magic square using the numbers 1 through 16.

6	1	15	12
16	11	5	2
3	8	10	13
9	14	4	7

Activity 18.5

The problem is for you to move . . . the same position as at the start.

Your students will probably recognize that the easiest way to see what makes this problem problematic is to use some objects to stand for the boxcars and the locomotive and then move those objects around. This playing with the problem may lead students to discover that the locomotive must make quite a number of passes around the triangular spur in order to get the boxcars into the the right places. Also, the number of passes the locomotive makes must be an odd number, because each trip around the spur makes the locomotive face the opposite direction. The most helpful clue for solving the problem is probably to discover where the boxcars need to be when the locomotive makes its final pass around the spur. Once the cars and locomotive are positioned as in the following picture, the problem is easily solved.

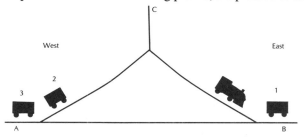

This problem is from *Teaching to Think* by Julius Boraas, (New York: Macmillan, 1920, pp. 159–160).

One Step Backwards

This section of the chapter warns students not to be so intent on moving forward toward the solution of a problem that they blind themselves to alternative approaches.

Activity 18.6

See if you can solve . . . in eleven steps.
Here are the eleven steps:

Start: MMM   B

       CCC

1.	MM CC	B M C	(A missionary and a cannibal bring the boat across.)
2.	MMM B CC	C	(The missionary brings it back.)
3.	MMM	B CCC	(Two cannibals bring the boat across.)
4.	MMM B C	CC	(One cannibal brings it back.)
5.	M C	B MM CC	(Two missionaries bring the boat across.)
6.	MM B CC	M C	(A missionary and a cannibal bring the boat back.)
7.	CC	B MMM C	(Two missionaries bring the boat across.)
8.	CCC B	MMM	(The cannibal brings it back.)
9.	C	B CC	(Two cannibals bring the boat across.)
10.	CC B	MMM C	(One cannibal brings it back.)
11.		B MMM CCC	(The two remaining cannibals bring the boat across.)

Activity 18.7

How can you use these cups . . . four ounces?
Here are the seven steps:

	8 oz.	5 oz.	3 oz.
Start:	8	0	0
1.	5	0	3
2.	5	3	0
3.	2	3	3
4.	2	5	1
5.	7	0	1
6.	7	1	0
7.	4	1	3

Eliminating Possibilities

This section of the chapter shows students that they don't always have to search for the solution in order to solve a problem. Sometimes, they can learn more by finding non-solutions.

The Sherlock Holmes excerpt is from *A Study in Scarlet and the Sign of Four*, by Sir Arthur Conan Doyle (New York: Berkley, 1975, pp. 172–174).

Activity 18.8

If you use the right procedure . . . What is that procedure?
The best approach is always to choose the middle number from the total pool of numbers. For example, the first guess should be fifty. If that guess is high, the next guess should be twenty-five, and so on. In this way, each guess eliminates half of the remaining possibilities. Because 2^7 is greater than 100, seven guesses will always find the number. If your students enjoy this problem, you might ask them how many guesses would be needed to get a number when the range is 1 to 1,000. (Because 2^{10} equals 1,024, ten guesses are all that are needed.)

Activity 18.9

Using the following information . . . decide what's wrong.
The VCR doesn't work because it isn't plugged in.

Rethinking: A Summary

To help your students begin this assignment, you might discuss with them how the main character in each of the examples could deal with the problem he or she faces. You could also have your students suggest other seemingly impossible situations.

Chapter 19: Talking About Problems

This chapter encourages students to think about the ways in which talking about problems both aid and complicate problem solving. The activities challenge students to recognize and bring together alternative points of view.

Working in a Group

This section of the chapter shows students how important it is, when they're working in a group, to share ideas—which means not only talking but also listening. The activity encourages students to be attentive.

Activity 19.1

Form a group . . . write and perform a short skit.
You might want to supervise this activity by checking the progress of the group at each step. Have them get your okay for their idea before they write the script.

Then, have them get your approval for the script before they practice it. Let the students work out their difficulties on their own as much as possible.

After your students perform their skits, you might have them discuss the problems of working in a group and the ways they found of overcoming those problems.

Finding Agreement

In this section of the chapter, students think about the ways in which personal interests complicate the discussion of social problems.

Activity 19.2

Form a group . . . decide what to do about the situation.

This activity gives students practice in seeing a problem from a variety of viewpoints and in keeping those viewpoints in mind while working on the problem.

Make sure your students understand that there is no easy answer to the problem, and they shouldn't expect to find one.

Talking to Yourself

This section of the chapter encourages students to be critical in their reflective thinking, to question and challenge their own ideas in the same way that they question and challenge the ideas of others.

The excerpt is from *How We Think* by John Dewey (Chicago: Regnery, 1971, [1933], pp. 70–71).

Activity 19.3

Do you keep the money or tell the clerk about the mistake?

Some of your students may feel compelled to write that, of course, they would return the money—that is, they may think the activity requests them to demonstrate a false sense of morality. Other students may not see the situation as problematic, because they feel no compunction to return the money. Both views miss the spirit of the activity, which is intended to give students an opportunity to talk through a private, hypothetical (but genuinely felt) problem. If the described situation does not seem to be a good one for your students, suggest a different one or have them come up with their own situation. Whatever situation your students write about, make sure they understand that they are not being tested to see if they can come up with the right answer. For the purpose of this activity, the process is more important than the result.

Rethinking: A Summary

If your students ask what qualifies as a ''surprising event,'' tell them that only they can decide. This assignment should give students a chance to think through something that genuinely puzzles them. Although the process of thinking through—talking out the questions with themselves—is the focus of the assignment, the realization that they, as students, can ask interesting, worthwhile questions is equally important.

Chapter 20: Understanding Analogies

This chapter gives students practice in applying the creative power of analogies to solving problems.

Sudden Insight

The first section of the chapter introduces the idea that the poetic insight of a metaphor can be the key not only to seeing a problem in a new light but also to finding a solution. The chapter also helps students realize their own capacity for metaphoric insight.

The story of the embryologist who was inspired by a painting was described in "Gene Screening: A Chance to Map Our Body's Future" by Peter Gorner and Ronald Kotulak (*Chicago Tribune*, Sunday, April 15, 1990, sec. 1, p. 1, 14).

Activity 20.1

As you reflect, freewrite . . . Look for metaphoric insights.

Your students may find this activity difficult because it lacks specific directions about what their final product is supposed to be. Encourage them to begin the activity on faith and not to worry about what they will come up with. Their insight may not seem so memorable as Verlinsky's, but they will probably be able to find in a moment of quiet reflection an unexpected connection with the day-to-day problems of their lives.

Activity 20.2

Write a brief description of the problem . . . some two-word metaphors that capture what the problem is about.

The problems that your students work with do not need to be the most serious problems they face. The aim of the activity is not to solve all the students' problems but to give them practice in drawing on metaphoric thinking.

If your students discuss the examples about loosening a screw in a hard-to-reach location, they may come up with such ideas as these:

- "knuckle scraper" suggests the need to wear gloves

- "slithering steel" suggests the idea of using a screwdriver with a flexible shaft like a snake used for clearing drains

- "double-jointed fingers" suggests using a screwdriver that bends at joints

Related Problems

This section of the chapter introduces the idea of using one problem to help solve another problem.

The Alexander Graham Bell quotation was reprinted in ''Synectics'' by William J. J. Gordon, in *Training Creative Thinking*, edited by Gary A. David and Joseph A. Scott (New York: Holt, Rinehart and Winston, 1971).

The dictator and radiation problems appear in *Problem Solving: A Cognitive Approach* by Hank Kahney (Philadelphia: Open University Press, 1986).

Activity 20.3

What solutions to the radiation problem . . . suggest?

When you discuss these problems with your students, stress the fact that different versions of the dictator problem suggest different solutions to the radiation problem. Understanding one problem can, by analogy, help them better understand a different problem.

1. The divided attack suggests the idea of using a direct ray in small doses that converge on the tumor from several angles.

2. The open-road attack suggests the idea of using a direct ray through an open passage, such as the esophagus, perhaps after covering it with a protective lining.

Getting Into the Problem

This section of the chapter focuses on another aspect of flexible thinking. It encourages students to study a problem from a wholly different (perhaps even nonhuman) point of view.

Activity 20.4

Imagine and act out . . . a bowl of soup.

You may need to remind your students that the main purpose of this activity is not to be funny or even to give the most identifiable performance (although both are desirable), but to experience the world from a radically different point of view.

Activity 20.5

Imagine that you are the tool . . . do you work?

If your students have done Activity 20.4, this one will not seem so strange. You might suggest that students begin the activity by narrating (from the first-person point of view of the tool) their experiences while cleaning the beach. After they get this inside view of the tool, your students may want to sketch it.

Activity 20.6

> *Imagine that you could go on a field trip . . . Understand the subject.*
> If your students would not think the "magic school bus" books too childish, you might have a few available for them to look at. You could also help your students get started on the activity by having them help you generate a list of possible topics. You might want to have your students write a story narrating what they discovered on their imaginary field trip.

Rethinking: A Summary

Examples are plentiful of poems of the sort that your students are to write for this assignment. You may want to share one or two, such as Edward Taylor's "Housewifery," Emily Dickinson's "Hope Is the Thing with Feathers," or Robert Frost's "The Road Not Taken." Make sure your students understand that their poem does not need to provide a neat solution to the problem they have in mind. A more realistic outcome is that, through their poems, students will come to grips with the problems they're writing about and feel that they understand those problems better than they did before.

Chapter 21: Researching

This chapter shows students that, for research to be an effective problem-solving strategy, it must be done with curiosity, persistence, open-mindedness, and attentiveness. The chapter introduces some of the kinds of problems that research can help solve.

Very Interesting

This section of the chapter focuses on how curiosity can provide the basis for meaningful research.

The story of Alexander Fleming is told in "Something Extraordinary" by Berton Roueché, in *Eleven Blue Men and Other Narratives of Medical Detection* (Boston: Little, Brown and Co., 1953).

Activity 21.1

> *Which ones do you think you should read . . . about the ones you've chosen?*
> Assure your students that there's no list of right answers for this activity. What matters is not which articles they choose but why they choose them. For instance, a student might choose the articles from *Senior Scholastic* and *Seventeen* in order to get an adolescent perspective. Someone else might be curious about why *Science* and *Science Digest* would contain articles about the Beatles. If your students can explain their choices with good reasons based on their own curiosity, then they've made the right choices.

Activity 21.2

Your job is to figure out . . . what features of the picture could help you solve this problem?

In order to figure out the occasion, the setting, and the date of the photograph, students might note the following clues: the expressions and the focus of the people suggest a parade or event; the dress of the children suggests Europe in the 1940s or 1950s; some of the men are wearing uniforms, which might be identified. In reality, the photo was taken shortly after World War II, as a new bell for war-damaged St. Stephen's Cathedral was being transported from Linz, Austria to the cathedral in Vienna. People lined the streets for this occasion.

Making Sure

This section of the chapter encourages students to take their curiosity out into the world and to be persistent in their research.

The story told by Rudyard Kipling appears in *The Creative Process: A Symposium*, edited by Brewster Ghiselin, (New York: new American Library, 1952).

Activity 21.3

Suppose you want to buy . . . give you the most certainty?

You may want to have your students work in groups on this activity. You could challenge them to see which group can produce the most or the best ideas. Remind your students to think not only about secondhand methods of research, such as checking *Consumer Reports* or asking friends about their stereos, but also about firsthand methods, such as listening to or examining stereos.

Activity 21.4

Using only a sheet of paper . . . What do you need to do?

To test this question, students need to make a paper airplane and try flying it with flaps up and with flaps down. If your students try this out, make sure they understand that they are to do more than play with their airplane. They need to observe the flights carefully and keep accurate records.

Getting Help

This section of the chapter shows students the variety of sources they might consult when doing research.

The story of how Ann Landers got her job was told in "A Woman of Letters," an interview with Ann Landers by Norma Libman in the *Chicago Tribune Magazine* (October 7, 1990, pp. 16ff).

Activity 21.5

For each of the problems . . . be most helpful? Why?
Here are some sample answers:

1. *Readers' Guide to Periodical Literature*

2. thesaurus; person with exceptional vocabulary

3. humane society; police department

4. check library for book on the subject; ask a friend

5. art gallery; check phone book for information about collectors

6. talk to people who work at the company

7. check library; write to schools; find out if the brothers and sisters of any friends have gone to a nearby college

Unnecessary Facts

This section of the chapter introduces the idea that research involves more than just collecting facts; those facts must be evaluated.

Activity 21.6

Construct a similar problem of your own. . . . don't give any more clues than are absolutely necessary.
    Make sure that your students understand that their aim is to create a puzzle with the minimum number of clues. The puzzle should be tricky but solvable.

Rethinking: A Summary

As you prepare your students for this assignment, you may want to discuss the purpose and structure of an essay that compares and contrasts. Make sure your students understand that they are not defining the two terms (though definition may be part of their essay); rather, they are showing how the two terms are alike and different. make sure also that your students understand that they should use their sources as means, not as ends. The purpose of the essay is not to present the sources but to use the sources to better understand the nature of *knowledge* and *wisdom*.

Part 4: Thinking Critically

This final part of the book introduces students to interpretation, logic, judgment, and evaluation. Whereas Part 2 deals with generating ideas and part 3 deals with applying ideas, Part 4 deals with reflecting on ideas to see what they mean, whether they are sensible, and whether they are believable. Much of this part of the book is concerned with the analysis of arguments. Make sure that your students understand that, in this sense, the word *argument* refers not to a disagreement but to a case, or an instance of logical reasoning in which evidence is used to draw a conclusion.

Chapter 22: Reading Between the Lines

This chapter encourages students to read (and listen) sensitively, paying attention not only to what is explicitly stated but also what is implied, assumed, or ignored.

Underlying Values

This section of the chapter shows students that in order to think critically about an argument or a point of view, they have to consider the values implicit in the argument.

The excerpt is from a speech given by William Wilberforce in the House of Commons on May 12, 1789, and can be found in *A Treasury of the World's Great Speeches*, edited by Houston Peterson (New York: Simon and Schuster, 1954, pp. 212–219).

Activity 22.1

What assumption . . . What value underlies the response of the spokesperson?
The reporter questioning the record company spokesperson seems to believe that dishonesty would be embarrassing. The spokesperson, on the other hand, seems to value profit above any other consideration.

Activity 22.2

Think about advertisements . . . What value do these ads most often appeal to?
Print ads would be easiest for your students to use because the pictures and the text can be studied with care. If students want to use television or radio ads, they'll need to take notes. Or, perhaps they could tape the ads.

If you think your students might have trouble discerning the values that underlie these ads, you might have them work in groups, or you could have the entire class study and talk together about three or four ads.

Unstated Assumptions

This section of the chapter encourages students to be more aware of the conclusions and beliefs that are taken for granted by writers and speakers.

Activity 22.3

What unstated assumptions does the argument depend on?
    The newspaper editorial (which is made up) assumes that education is the key ingredient in a country's economic success and that graduation is a key ingredient in a successful education.

Activity 22.4

What unstated assumption lies behind the following assertion?
    The argument assumes that rats and mice have some insight into nutrition.

Activity 22.5

At the beginning of each round . . . affect your own strategy?
    In this game, players will probably assume that their opponent will deliberately make confusing and unpredictable choices. In other words, opponents will tend not to show the same side repeatedly and not to follow a pattern. Sophisticated game players may note that, once a player gets in the lead, it is to that player's advantage to choose a side randomly—if the player wins half the rounds, he or she will remain in the lead.

Knowing Your Own Prejudices

This section of the chapter encourages students to be aware of the ways in which their own prejudices can interfere with their ability to think critically. Some of your students may think of the word *prejudice* as having to do only with racial attitudes. Explain to them that the prejudices discussed in this section of the chapter are any ideas or beliefs held without evidence or without the holder being willing to question them.
    The ''Sunday Morning'' episode aired August 4, 1990.

Activity 22.6

Jot down your views about the sentencing of criminals . . . causes you to rethink them.
    Your students may have a variety of views—from concerns about the ''soft'' treatment of criminals to fears that the law is too harsh. Make sure they get their views on paper before they read the excerpt. Emphasize that the purpose of the activity is not to prove or disprove any view but to discover how prejudices can interfere with the ability to think critically. You might ask your students to consider whether their response to those portions of the excerpt that agreed with

their views differed from their response to those portions that disagreed. Are they inclined to believe the former and disbelieve the latter?

The excerpt is from "Doing the Crime, Not the Time" by Andrea Sachs (*Time*, September 11, 1989).

Activity 22.7

Jot down your views about what such movies teach people . . . cause you to rethink them.

Your students may have a variety of views, including concerns about gratuitous violence, exploitation of women, or even what they see as the unwarranted complaints of antiviolence activists. As with Activity 22.6, the aim is to get students thinking about how their own prejudices can make it hard to think critically about views that agree or disagree with their own. You may want to ask your students to consider whether it's more difficult for them to think fairly and critically about views that agree with their own or about views that disagree with their own.

The excerpt is from " 'Reel' vs. Real Violence" by John Russo (*Newsweek*, February 19, 1990).

Standards of Evaluation

This section of the chapter makes students more aware of the standards they apply when they make judgments.

Activity 22.8

What qualities . . . in evaluating the following?
Your students might choose the following qualities:

1. *family car*: roomy, inexpensive to buy, inexpensive to operate, sturdy, safe

2. *bicycle for use in a Midwestern city:* single gear, portable, able to handle bumps and curbs

3. *science-fiction movie:* imaginative, uses elements of life today to see into future, deals with current issues or problems

4. *pair of everyday shoes*: practical, comfortable, sturdy

5. *loaf of bread*: fresh, tasty, chewy

6. *painting:* color, balance, proportion, theme

7. *personal computer*: easy to use, adaptable

8. *rap song*: rhyme, invention, rhythm, popular theme

9. *newspaper*: thorough, objective, informed

10. *camera for trip to mountains*: portable, wide-angle lens

Activity 22.9

Decide which way is better for the purpose given.

You may want to tell your students that one of each pair is a quotation. Of course, the aim of the activity is not to have students guess which is the genuine quotation. The aim is to give them an opportunity to discuss why one quotation is better than the other (for the purpose): what standards justify their choice? Here are sample answers:

1. b. is from Lincoln's second inaugural address; the elevated language better suits the occasion.

2. a. is from Lincoln's Gettysburg Address; the elevated language and Biblical construction suit the occasion.

3. a. is from a radio speech by Winston Churchill following Dunkirk; the repetition of location drives home the point of determination.

4. a. is from *An Ideal Husband*, by Oscar Wilde; the paradox adds to the wittiness.

5. a. is from Woodrow Wilson's address to Congress asking for war in 1917; democracy does not force itself on people.

6. b. is by H. A. R. Buller, quoted in *The Art of the Limerick* by Cyril Bibby (Hamden, Conn.: Archon Books, 1978); the reference to relativity and the playfulness of the form create humor.

Rethinking: A Summary

You may want to read the excerpt with your students to make sure they understand what it's about. Stress that the aim of the essay is not for them simply to say that they like or dislike the excerpt. They are to consider in their essay the values and assumptions that underlie Machiavelli's point of view, and to consider his views without letting their own prejudices interfere with their ability to think critically. This doesn't mean they have to agree with him. It only means that they should think carefully about what he has to say before they decide whether they agree with him.

The excerpt is from *The Prince*, translated by T. G. Bergin (AHM Publishing Corp., 1947, p. 48).

Chapter 23: Induction

This chapter introduces the concept of inductive reasoning. Ordinarily, induction is described as the process of reasoning from the particular to the general. This is the definition given by Aristotle, who said that an inductive argument demonstrates that a universal conclusion is implicit in particular premises.

Rather than talking about the particular and the general, however, this chapter focuses on the implicit nature of an inductive conclusion. To think critically about arguments, students must concentrate on the process by which the conclusion is derived from the premises. The chapter, therefore, gets students thinking about the logic of inductive reasoning.

Drawing Conclusions

This section of the chapter gives students the materials to construct an inductive argument.

Activity 23.1

Using the sonnet . . . construct an inductive argument about the date of the sonnet.

Read the sonnet with your students to make sure they understand what it's about. You may also want to give your students more background information about John Milton and his times. (*The Oxford Companion to English Literature,* 5th ed., edited by Margaret Drabble, contains an informative article.)

Sonnet XIX was certainly composed after Milton became blind and probably not long after. The reference to his being halfway through life suggests he may have been 42 if he was thinking of his father who lived to be 84. This would place the poem at the end of 1651 or early in 1652. It certainly came before he began *Paradise Lost* (1657). The tone of the poem—the sense of being useless— suggests he is feeling his loss strongly.

Are You Convinced?

This section of the chapter gets students thinking about how they can tell whether the premises of an inductive argument warrant the conclusion.

The article is "The Lesson of Rock and Roll" by Jerry Adler (*Newsweek,* January 29, 1990, p. 76).

Activity 23.2

Suppose you are a history teacher. Will you play . . . Why or why not?

Your students may or may not find Adler's argument convincing. Make sure that, whatever their decision about playing the song, they show why Adler's argument is or is not convincing. Some of your students may agree with Adler's argument but think of alternative reasons for playing the record in a history class.

Activity 23.3

Rate the arguments from the weakest to the strongest.

Here is a sample answer:

The weakest argument is 1, because monthly patterns of weather tell nothing about daily weather. Next weakest is probably 3, because a week-old prediction is of little value. However, the reason for the umbrella—protecting the books—offers something 1 does not. Next might be 4, because the prediction is timely and supposedly reliable. The strongest argument is 2, because the timeliness and consensus reinforce the authority of the prediction (although all three forecasters may have gotten their prediction from the same source).

Activity 23.4

Which of these conclusions is most strongly supported by the premises?
Here are sample answers:

- None of the statements support conclusion *a*.

- Conclusion *b* is supported by statements 4 and 5, but questioned by 6 and 7 (though 4 and 5 may be seen as more reliable).
- Conclusion *c* is made questionable by the conflicts in testimony: if statements 5 and 6 are both accurate, the witnesses may well be talking about different phenomena.
- Conclusion *d* is supported by the contradictions and is the strongest of the conclusions (though far from certain).

The statements are derived from an article headlined "Strange Light Reported over Eastern U.S." in the *Chicago Tribune* (January 28, 1990, sec. 1, p. 6).

What's Missing?

This section of the chapter encourages students to ask themselves whether the premises of an inductive argument are incomplete and therefore inconclusive.

The market research was conducted by the Chrysler Corporation and announced by Lee Iacocca in a television commercial campaign conducted during May 1990. The events were reported in the *New York Times* (Sunday, May 13, 1990, sec. 4, p. 5).

Activity 23.5

Explain why the premises . . . too weak to make the conclusions convincing.
Here are some questions that point out potentially significant information the premises do not mention:

1. What features do the cars have? How have they been used? What condition are they in?

2. How well do other students who take the course do? Is it surprising for these students to do well? Would they have done well anyway?

3. How unusual are the conditions? How many planets are there likely to be in the universe?

4. How do the players compare in games played, at bats, home runs, runs batted in, and fielding? What positions do they play?

5. What was Felicia's position in the race when she fell? How fast was she going? How fast were the others going? How many people were in the race?

6. What was the scale on which these GPAs were figured? What courses did the students take? How did their schools compare? What extracurricular activities were they involved in?

7. How were these comments collected? Were other comments not used? Who made these comments?

8. How many cats do not do any of these things? Are these the only instances of misbehavior the cats ever committed?

Rethinking: A Summary

You may want to read and discuss the excerpt with your students. They should understand that the writer's inductive conclusion is that "an expanded road network" is needed to solve the nation's "traffic woes." As your students examine the argument supporting this conclusion, they'll need to think about both the premises that the writer offers and the alternative solutions that the writer doesn't consider. If there are better solutions to the traffic woes than an expanded road network, then the inductive conclusion does not follow, and the writer's call for more money is not supported.

The excerpt is from "Hassle-Free Driving Soothes Nerves, Saves Gas" by J. Kay Aldous (*Home and Away*, March/April 1991, p. 10).

Chapter 24: Deduction

This chapter introduces deductive reasoning—arguments that lead to a necessary conclusion. The chapter shows students how to tell the difference between valid and invalid arguments.

Syllogisms

This section of the chapter shows students how to construct a syllogism and how to use a Venn diagram to test whether a syllogism is valid.

Activity 24.1

A. *Is the argument valid? Does it prove . . . tuxedos?*
   Yes. Those jugglers who overlap the category of musicians are not tuxedo wearers.

B. *Suppose the following . . . Is it valid?*
   No. The premises do not tell whether any of the jugglers overlap the tuxedo-wearing group.

C. *Can more than one valid . . . same set of premises? Why or why not?*
   No. When the middle term—the one that appears in both premises—is dropped out, there are only two terms left for the conclusion to relate, and they relate in only one way.

Activity 24.2

Decide whether the following arguments . . . show the relationships.

1. Invalid

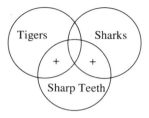

2. Valid

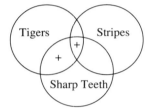

3. Invalid

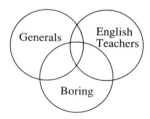

4. Valid

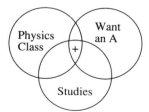

5. Invalid

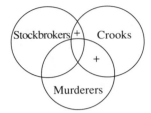

6. Valid

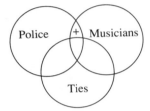

7. Valid

8. Valid

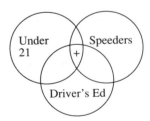

Activity 24.3

Write down the premises . . . Venn diagram.
Only serpents have long necks and eat eggs.
Alice has a long neck and eats eggs.
Therefore, Alice is a serpent.

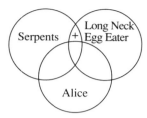

The diagram shows that the argument, if constructed this way, is valid. It might also be constructed in another way:

> Serpents have long necks and eat eggs.
> Alice has a long neck and eats eggs.
> Therefore, Alice is a serpent.

This argument, which requires a different diagram, is invalid:

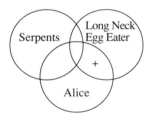

The Pigeon seems to have the former in mind.

Chains of Syllogisms

This section of the chapter introduces arguments that consist of groups, or chains, of syllogisms. The chapter helps students recognize syllogistic reasoning even when it is not formally laid out.

Carroll's sorites, or chains of syllogisms, are from *Symbolic Logic* by Lewis Carroll, 4th ed. (London: Macmillan and Company).

Activity 24.4

A. *Write the premises . . . careless.*

> Only a careless man would carry a valuable watch in the same pocket with coins and other metal objects.
>
> The owner of this watch carried it in the same pocket with coins and other metal objects.
>
> The owner of this watch was careless.

B. *Write the premises . . . needed money.*

Only pawnbrokers make pin marks inside a watch case.
This watch has several pin marks.
This watch has been pawned several times.

This watch has been pawned several times.
Only people who need money pawn their watch.
The owner of this watch needed money.

C. *Write the premises . . . drunkard.*
Only a drunkard digs grooves around a watch's keyhole.
This watch has grooves around the keyhole.
The owner of this watch was a drunkard.

D. *Are Holmes's arguments valid . . . Why or why not?*
The arguments are valid, though all the universal premises (the general
statements) are questionable.

Activity 24.5

What conclusion . . . premises?
The only articles of food that my doctor allows me are such as are not very
rich.
Wedding cake is always very rich.
My doctor does not allow me wedding cake.

My doctor does not allow me wedding cake.
My doctor allows me all articles of food that are suitable for supper.
Wedding cake is not suitable for supper.

Wedding cake is not suitable for supper.
Nothing that agrees with me is unsuitable for supper.
Wedding cake does not agree with me.

If . . . Then . . .

This section of the chapter introduced deductive reasoning based on propositions. Students should see how a valid conclusion can be drawn from an if/then proposition.

The *Raiders of the Lost Ark* argument appears in "Teaching Thinking and Problem Solving" by John D. Bransford, Robert D. Sherwood, and Tom Sturdevant, in *Teaching Thinking Skills*, edited by Joan Boykoff Baron and Robert J. Sternberg (New York: W. H. Freeman and Co., 1987).

Activity 24.6

Write out . . . premises and conclusions.

If the lawyer had seen two red stickers, he would have known what color
sticker he had.

He did not know what color sticker he had.
Therefore, he did not see two red stickers.

If the doctor had seen a red sticker on the philosopher, she would have
    known that she had a blue sticker (because the lawyer's conclusion
    shows that either the doctor or the philosopher must have a blue
    sticker).
The doctor did not know she had a blue sticker.
Therefore, she did not see a red sticker on the philosopher.

The philosopher announced she was wearing a blue sticker.

Activity 24.7

*Write out . . . premises and a conclusion. Is the argument valid? Do you find it
convincing? Why or why not?*

If anyone could teach virtue, the Sophists or the noblest Athenians could.
If they could teach virtue, they would.
The students of the Sophists and the children of the noblest Athenians
    have not all been taught virtue.
Therefore, virtue cannot be taught.

The argument is valid, though it is possible that *teaching* in the first two premises
means something different from *taught* in the third. Students may or may not find the
argument convincing. Encourage them to discuss their reasons for accepting it or not.

Activity 24.8

A. *Tell whether . . . valid or invalid. Explain your answers.*

1. Invalid. Other things may have caused the car to stop running.

2. Invalid. The car may be broken.

3. Invalid. Other things can cause a baby to cry.

4. Invalid. Nice teachers assign homework, too.

B. *What do the examples . . . deductive arguments?*

   Neither affirming the consequent (the *then* part) nor denying the antecedent (the
if part) yields a valid conclusion.

Rethinking: A Summary

Discuss the case to be sure your students understand the basic facts. Stress that in their
essay they are to explain the argument of the majority decision before they discuss
whether the argument is valid and whether its premises are sound. The argument your
students find should be something like this:

If all citizens were pacifists, the country and the Constitution would be lost.
The country and the Constitution cannot be allowed to disappear.
Therefore, all citizens cannot be pacifists.

This argument is valid, but the proposition on which it is based is suspect, a point that was made by Oliver Wendell Holmes, Jr., in his dissenting opinion, reprinted in *The Norton Reader*, edited by Arthur M. Eastman, et al. (New York: W. W. Norton and Co., 1965, pp. 769–771).

Chapter 25: Nonsense

This chapter shows students several ways in which evidence, details, and facts can be used to mislead. The activities offer a variety of examples of fallacies, propaganda, and deceptions.

Your students might enjoy the humorous look at this subject in the short story "Love Is a Fallacy," by Max Shulberg.

False Impressions

This section of the chapter shows students how ambiguity and misrepresentation can lead to false conclusions.

Activity 25.1

What impression . . . different from that first impression?

1. *Great* seems at first to be a description, but it is only part of the name.
2. The thirty-minute workout tape is at first made to seem longer by suggesting that it accomplishes as much as a ninety-minute workout—the tape is still only thirty minutes long.
3. The pet food at first seems special because it is "scientific," but what does that mean? Presumably it means that nutrition is considered by the company that makes the food, which is probably true of all pet foods.
4. The price of the car is made to seem less at first by the emphasis on "under" $18,000. In fact, the difference between the price and $18,000 is negligible. And when other elements of buying a car are added in, the price may be much higher.
5. "Thinning hair" means that hair is falling out so that the head of hair as a whole is thinner. Making thicker those hairs that remain won't help.

Activity 25.2

Who do you think . . . group opposing it?

The consumer group sent out the information. Although the first column shows monthly rates, column 2 is based on annual rates and column 4 on 5-year rates.

The precision of the figures is nonsense, because they are based on estimated use. The derivation of the figures (the actual terms of the rate increase) are not explained and can't even be interpreted. The aim is to make the rate increase seem as large as possible: saying that the annual increase (for an average monthly bill of $20) will be $38.50 sounds much worse than saying that the monthly bill will go up to about $23 (based on the 16 percent increase from column 3).

Activity 25.3

Explain . . . not really valid.

To say that no one can predict compatibility with another person for life means that differences can arise between people and that it's unreasonable to imagine that anyone could choose a person with whom he or she could live without disagreements. But to say that people who aren't compatible can't live together uses a different sense of *compatible*: it means that people have to get along if they're going to live together, but this "getting along" doesn't necessarily mean never disagreeing. In this sense, compatible people can have problems that they work through together.

Activity 25.4

What's wrong . . . argument?

In general, the argument is guilty of the fallacy called *post hoc, ergo propter hoc*. The argument assumes that, because one event followed another, the first is the cause of the second. Although the argument seems to be talking about cause and effect, it's actually discussing events that are not causally related (and probably unrelated altogether).

Missing Premises

In this section of the chapter, students analyze incomplete arguments to find the premises that are left unstated. The aim is to make students less susceptible to arguments that are deceptive because they are elliptical.

Activity 25.5

What would the second premise . . . Why or why not?

The given first premise is

Our brand is thicker than any other leading brand.

The following premise could be added to make an inductive argument leading to the conclusion, "You should buy our brand":

Thick ketchup is better than thin ketchup.

The premise is rather vague and obviously not true at the extreme: ketchup in a solid lump would not be desirable. Whether students find the argument convincing will depend on their interpretation of the premise and on what they have in mind when they imagine *thick* and *thin*. At best, the argument is suggestive.

Activity 25.6

Write out the arguments . . . convincing.
  Sample answers:
1. To have a lot of energy, you need to eat high-energy food.
   A car's use of fuel is analogous to a person's use of food.
   Our brand of gasoline is the highest in energy.
   You want your car to have the highest possible energy. Therefore, you should buy our gasoline.

All of the premises are questionable and the conclusion weak.

2. If you're planning to make a lot of long-distance calls, you'll spend less using our service than you would if you used another company's service.
   You are planning to make a lot of long-distance calls.
   Therefore, you should use our service.

The argument fails to make clear how many calls would have to be made before the cost of changing service would be made up by the savings. That is, how many is "a lot of long-distance calls"? Also, the fact that making these calls will cost you money, not save your money, is hidden by talk of savings. You'll only save money if you were planning to make the requisite number of phone calls anyway (premise 2), and that may not be true.

3. A state's attorney should get convictions in most of the cases that are prosecuted.
   The candidate did not get convictions in most of the cases she prosecuted.
   Therefore, she is not a good state's attorney.

The first premise is questionable. What is an average rate of conviction? Certainly, it would be wrong in a fair judicial system to think that all prosecutions would result in conviction; in that event, trials wouldn't be necessary.

4. If you don't drink Cola Light, you'll drink something else that has more calories.
   You want to limit your intake of calories.
   Therefore, you should drink Cola Light.

There's no reason whatever to find the first premise convincing, so the argument seems extremely weak.

5. You want to drive fast on the open highway.
   Our car will allow you to drive fast on the open highway.
   Therefore, you should buy our car.

No car can do away with speed limits or with other traffic. The second premise is false.

6. If you don't use our breath mints, people will avoid you.
   You don't want people to avoid you.
   Therefore, you should use our breath mint.

In essence, this argument is a case of denying the consequent (the *then* part of the first premise). No valid conclusion can be drawn from such an argument.

Activity 25.7

Find an ad . . . more or less persuasive.
   Students should describe the ad fully and accurately, draw out the implied argument, and show what premises are missing from the ad as it is presented. It would be helpful for students to present this work orally, perhaps to the entire class. Those who are listening should consider whether there are alternative, likelier readings of the ad.

Begging the Question

This section of the chapter gives students practice in detecting circular arguments.

Activity 25.8

Explain . . . begging the question.
   Sample answers:
1. The quality of Muffler City's work is taken for granted, though that is precisely what consumers may wonder about.
2. Snack crackers are *only* eaten because they taste good. The ad takes the tastiness of oat Fiber Crunchies for granted.
3. The assumption is that this car is as good as cars get: one can't "move up" from this car.
4. Since everyone wants the lowest prices, the valid conclusion is that it is better to shop at Al's. But why is it better? The premise assumes that Al's prices are the lowest, but no evidence is offered to support that assumption.
5. The tippler's explanation is a classic circle in which drinking is both the cause and the cure. The fact that he is a "tippler" is thus taken for granted.
       The excerpt is from *The Little Prince* by Antoine de Saint-Exupéry, translated by Katherine Woods (New York: Harcourt Brace and World, 1943, pp. 50–52).
6. Hal uses the assumption that a woman must lose the election as a reason for people not to vote for her (which is, of course, how elections are lost). This circular argument begs the question of whether a woman could be elected President.

Rethinking: A Summary

Read and discuss the excerpt to make sure your students understand the circumstances and point of the speech. In their essays, they may note that the speech uses vague and ambiguous language (*traitor, loyalty, sacred pledges, agitators, destroyers,* etc.), incomplete arguments (he who rises against Germany is a traitor; [he who opposes me rises against Germany]; these people opposed me: therefore, they are traitors), and question-begging (the conclusion that trials are not needed is based on the premise that the men were traitors, which is the charge that the trial was supposed to investigate).

An excerpt from the speech and some background information about it appear in *A Treasury of the World's Great Speeches*, edited by Houston Peterson (New York: Simon and Schuster, 1954, pp. 755–60).

Chapter 26: Evaluating

This chapter is a summing up—a final exam of sorts, but only in the sense that the chapter encourages students to pull together everything that has gone before. Evaluating incorporates not only the critical thinking discussed in Part 4 but also the creative thinking and problem solving discussed earlier in the book.

You may want to use these activities as you used the Rethinking assignments. Or, you could use them as bases for discussions—either in small groups or with the whole class.

Activity 26.1

Which one should . . . explaining your choice.

You may want to read both poems with your students and discuss them. If you think it will help your students, you might also discuss possible reasons for choosing one poem over the other—the imagery, the versification, the appropriateness of the theme, the tone. Any aspect of the poem might provide a basis for choice—if that aspect can be connected to the interests of high school students or to a concept of what they ought to read.

Activity 26.2

Write a letter . . . explain and defend your choice.

It may help if you discuss with your students possible choices. You could list their suggestions on the chalkboard. Encourage them to listen carefully and multiple times to the music they choose before they attempt to write about it. Their letter should be specific in talking about the qualities of the music and about what this music says about human life, human culture, human values. This doesn't mean that the essay must be heavy or somber. The desire to laugh and play are human characteristics, too.

Activity 26.3

Is Vivian . . . in your character sketch.

Students may find Vivian (from Oscar Wilde's essay "The Decay of Lying," which can be found in *The Norton Anthology of English Literature*, vol. 2, edited by M. H. Abrams [New York: W. W. Norton and Co., 1962]) to be a surprising person: when he asserts that all people are indeed equal, he finds the thought depressing. You may want to discuss what Vivian means by the "brotherhood of man" before your students begin writing their sketch.

Activity 26.4

Do you think this person . . . recommending him.

To do this assignment, your students have to understand and evaluate Frazer's view of primitive people—in particular his beliefs that their lack of experience and tradition makes them different in kind from civilized people and that they live in a more fearful, less reliable world. If your students do not share this view, they will probably question Frazer's suitability for the job. If they do share this view of "primitives," they may find Frazer to be a thoughtful and experienced candidate. Or, they may object to him on other grounds.

The excerpt is from *The Golden Bough: A Study in Magic and Religion* (New York: Macmillan, 1951, pp. 373–74).

Activity 26.5

Judging by the following excerpt . . . statement of your view.

Students need to determine whether this excerpt speaks to them. Is Tacitus interesting? Does he seem to be just in his presentation and keen-eyed in his judgment? Does he have anything to say to people living at the end of the twentieth century? Is there value in hearing out his surprisingly different point of view?

The excerpt is from *The Complete Works of Tacitus*, edited by Moses Hadas (New York: The Modern Library, 1942, pp 380–81).

Activity 26.6

Which excerpt . . . in an essay of your own.

This activity touches on one of the most puzzling of questions: what is humor? Because humor is so taken for granted, however, your students may not see at first what the activity is asking them to think about. Make sure that your students understand that the excerpts are different in two ways: one, their form is different—excerpt I is a demonstration and excerpt II, an explanation—and, two, their point is different—excerpt I shows how closely one's sense of self is identified with one's sense of humor, while excerpt II says that humor is the other side of sorrow. These points are not contradictory, but they are different. Your students should reflect on their own sense of humor (not only what makes them laugh but also what the point of laughter is) before they try to evaluate what Leacock has to say.

These excerpts are from *Further Foolishness* (Toronto: McClelland and Stewart, 1968 [1916], pp. 157, 164).

Bibliography

The following titles suggest the range of approaches to the study and teaching of thinking. Several of the books listed have extensive bibliographies for those who are interested in exploring the subject in greater depth.

Bruner, Jerome. 1966. *Toward a Theory of Instruction.* Cambridge, Mass.: Harvard Univ. Press.
 Bruner analyzes a number of curricula and classroom instructional strategies. His premise is that "any idea or problem or body of knowledge can be presented in a form simple enough so that any particular learner can understand it in a recognizable form." From this viewpoint, all instruction is a matter of finding the "way of thought" that underlies the subject matter.

Dewey, John. 1971 (1933). *How We Think.* Chicago: Regnery.
 This book is a philosophical examination of reflective thinking. Though the book is concerned with what Dewey calls "reflection," it shows his concern with active thought—thought that begins with needs born out of experience and that culminates in an action or conviction that resolves the tensions and perplexities that initiate the process.

Douglas, Mary. 1986. *How Institutions Think.* Syracuse, N.Y.: Syracuse Univ. Press.
 This book is a sociological/anthropological study of how society, culture, institutions determine what is possible (or likely) for individuals to think. The book is a reminder that individualistic approaches to teaching thinking miss an important dimension of the process.

Erskine, John. 1921 (1915). *The Moral Obligation to Be Intelligent.* New York: Duffield and Co.
 This collection of five essays on English literature asks whether intelligence is a virtue, whether goodness is a separate quality from wisdom.

Flack, Jerry D. 1990. *Mystery and Detection: Thinking and Problem Solving with the Sleuths.* Englewood, Colo.: Teachers Idea Press.
 This book is a collection of activities (with many lists of resources) centered on the theme of mystery and detection. Most of the activities are aimed at high school students.

Gardner, Howard. 1983. *Frames of Mind.* New York: Basic Books.
 This book describes the seven "intelligences," or forms of thinking, that Gardner believes have developed in human beings. These are logical-mathematical, linguistic, musical, spatial, bodily-kinesthetic, interpersonal, and intrapersonal.

Ghiselin, Brewster, ed. 1952. *The Creative Process: A Symposium.* New York: New
American Library.
This anthology contains forty excerpts by such people as Einstein, Mozart, van
Gogh, Wordsworth, Amy Lowell, and Katherine Anne Porter. Each excerpt is con-
cerned with the writer's inspiration or working out of a creative idea.

Golub, Jeff, and the Committee on Classroom Practices. 1986. *Activities to Promote
Critical Thinking.* Urbana, Ill.: National Council of Teachers of English.
This is a collection of twenty-eight language-arts activities designed to promote
critical thinking. Most of the activities are intended for high school or college English classes.

Marzano, Robert J., Ronald S. Brandt, Carolyn Sue Hughes, Beau Fly Jones, Barbara
S. Presseisen, Stuart C. Rankin, and Charles Suhor. 1988. *Dimensions of Thinking:
A Framework for Curriculum and Instruction.* Alexandria, Va.: Association for Su-
pervision and Curriculum Development.
This book is intended to help teachers design their own curriculum materials that
will highlight thinking. It distinguishes critical and creative thinking, identifies eight
thinking processes, and describes twenty-one thinking skills as well as discusses the
relationships between content-area knowledge and thinking. This book contains an
extensive list of references.

McPeck, John E. 1990. *Teaching Critical Thinking: Dialogue and Dialectic.* New
York: Routledge.
This book contains two parts. In the first, McPeck offers his view that there are
no general critical thinking skills because all thinking is thinking about something in
particular. The best way to teach critical thinking, therefore, is within the standard
subjects, the liberal arts curriculum. In the second part of the book, three educational
researchers respond to McPeck's views.

Paulos, John Allen. 1990 (1985). *I Think, Therefore, I Laugh: An Alternative Approach
to Philosophy.* New York: Vintage Books.
Advanced students, especially those interested in mathematics or philosophy,
will enjoy this books' numerous jokes, stories, puzzles, and anecdotes, all of which
illustrate or shed light on some of the enduring philosophical questions (and on the
subject of thinking). The prominent characters in the book are Ludwig Wittgenstein,
Lewis Carroll, Bertrand Russell, and Groucho Marx.

Plato. 1961. *Meno.* Translated by W. K. C. Guthrie. In *The Collected Dialogues of
Plato,* edited by Edith Hamilton and Huntington Cairns. Princeton: Princeton Univ.
Press.
This Socratic dialogue (available in many other editions) deals with the differ-
ence between knowledge and opinion, with the way in which learning occurs, and
with Socrates' belief that knowledge and virtue are one. The dialogue also offers an

interesting look at the Socratic method. Advanced students might find the dialogue readable and interesting.

Schrag, Frances. 1988. *Thinking in School and Society.* New York: Routledge.

Schrag argues that thinking is not a skill but the character trait he calls ''thoughtfulness.'' He describes alternative school settings that he believes would encourage the practice of thoughtfulness. This book contains an extensive list of references.

Smith, Frank. 1990. *to think.* New York: Teachers College Press.

Smith writes about what he calls ''commonplace thinking,'' the thinking that everyone does all day long. This is not, he says, ''a set of acquired skills, but rather a matter of experience, of understanding the requirements and conventions of particular subject matters.'' Smith attempts to show that remembering, understanding, learning, and thinking are all one activity, as are thinking creatively and thinking critically. This book contains an extensive list of references.